ARE YOU THE **World's** NEXT TOP **LEADER**

40 QUESTIONS
EVERY LEADER MUST ASK
BEFORE THEY LEAD IN THE
21ST CENTURY

WRITTEN BY
JOSHUA FREDENBURG

CONTENTS

ACKNOWLEDGEMENTS

There are so many people that I would love to thank for this book, but the first person that I must thank for this project is God, for giving me the strength, passion, and wisdom necessary to write another book that is geared towards impacting the lives of others. The second person that I would like to thank is the entire Biola University Masters of Arts in Organizational Leadership Program for igniting the passion in me to try to inspire, empower, and develop great leaders within our world. The third person I would like to thank is the entire Cottonwood Leadership College for supporting and providing with me with a life changing experience that really inspired me to write this book on leadership. And lastly, I would like to thank my family, daughter, friends, mentors, other leadership experts and colleagues, Circle of Change Leadership Conference family, and all the people who helped me make this book a reality. You are all very much appreciated for your support, inspiration, and motivation!

INTRODUCTION
WHERE THE JOURNEY BEGAN

Over the past one hundred years, as our nation has seen an evolution in different types of leaders from one generation to the next, the definition of leadership has evolved as well. According to certain leadership experts, in the first three decades of the twentieth century, leadership was defined as the ability to impress the will of the leader on those led and induce obedience, respect, loyalty, and cooperation. In the 1930s, leadership was viewed more as influence versus domination, while in the 1940s, men and women who studied leadership began to define it as the behavior of an individual while involved in directing group activities. By the 1950s, the three themes that dominated leadership were: continuance of group theory, leadership as a relationship that develops shared goals, and effectiveness, which is defined as the ability to influence overall group effectiveness.

Following this evolution of leadership during the first fifty years of the twentieth century came a new definition of leadership in 1960. This new definition described leadership as a behavior that influences people toward shared goals. Even though these definitions all captured aspects of leadership, in 1978 James MacGregor Burns, in his book entitled Leadership, put forth one of the most important definitions of leadership: "Leadership is the reciprocal process of mobilizing by persons with certain motives and values, various economic, political, and other resources, in a context of competition and conflict, in order to realize goals independently or mutually held by both leaders and followers." Ultimately, according to various leadership experts, once Burns established this definition, scholars of leadership began to realize that multiple definitions of leadership revolved around influence, traits, transformation, and leaders getting people to do what they desired to have done in a specific situation. Although these definitions and characteristics of leadership have continued to evolve since that time, I would agree with the definition of leadership put forth by Peter Northouse in Leadership: Theory and Practice, which is the process whereby an individual influences a group of individuals to achieve a common goal.

Although we have more leadership development programs than ever before, many individuals in America still believe we have a leadership crisis in all aspects of our society and culture. One of reasons these men and women believe we have leadership crisis in America is that certain individuals believe that leaders are more concerned about elections, deals, titles, bonuses, bailouts, and profits than the well-being of the people they serve. These leadership critics also believe that the essence of transformational leadership has been lost as a result of greed, fear, selfishness, lack of compassion, division among others, unethical behavior, and a lack of concern for the future of our nation and world. And a final reason is that these people who have become extremely concerned about the state of leadership in America believe that a majority of people who desire to become leaders are wannabes who want the benefits, prestige, accolades, respect, dignity, and power that come with leadership—without ever developing the courage, humility, wisdom, love, integrity, character, heart, purpose, resilience, values, and leadership skills necessary to become great leaders in the twenty-first century.

Although I agree with various men and women who make the assertion that we have a leadership crisis in America, I believe there are still some amazing leaders. I also believe that thousands of future leaders can emerge into powerful leaders of the twenty-first century with the right leadership training. Therefore, I have made it one of my missions over the past few years to develop a leadership book that encompasses fifteen years of leadership training and research, hundreds of keynote speeches and workshops on the topic of leadership, countless personal experiences as a leader over the past twenty years, and a multitude of discussions with successful leaders around the world. Drawing from this breadth of training, research, and experience, I have developed forty questions that I believe every leader must ask themselves before they aspire to become one of the world's next top leaders.

Throughout this book, emerging and seasoned leaders will have the opportunity to reflect, digest, discuss, and learn about forty specific leadership qualities that every individual must consider before they become a leader in the twenty-first century. Also, men and women who aspire to become one of the world's next top leaders will discover the leader within and uncover specific leadership skills that will enable them to evolve into effective relational leaders. In addition, emerging and seasoned leaders will find out the keys to becoming effective operational leaders and learn how to create a strong spiritual foundation for leadership success in the twenty-first century. My hope, with these different sets of leadership questions, is that emerging and seasoned leaders who take the time to read, reflect, and digest the information in this book will apply it to their lives and allow the powerful insights discussed in this book to help them make a positive impact on their community, nation, and world!

CHAPTER ONE
THE INNER LEADER

Approximately three years ago, I heard an international speaker by the name of Noel Jones say, "Every time a child is born, a solution is brought into the world." In essence, according to Mr. Jones, every time a baby boy or girl is brought into the world, this adorable creation not only brings happiness, love, peace, and joy to others, but this amazing child also comes to earth with amazing inner qualities that are designed to help the child positively impact the lives of others. Ultimately, in order for these powerful and unique inner qualities to manifest, the child must discover, investigate, and develop these powerful attributes that are inside every individual who desires to become one of the world's next top leaders.

To help you discover these amazing leadership qualities that have been placed within you, I have developed eleven specific questions in this first chapter of the book to help you discover the leader within. My hope is that these eleven questions will not only help you uncover and reflect on some of the unknown aspects of leadership potential that have been placed within you, but that the questions will help you develop a set of leadership skills that you will need to cultivate in order to evolve into one of the world's next top leaders!

LEADERSHIP QUESTION #1
Do you possess self-awareness?

Throughout my life, I have learned many different lessons about leadership. One of the most important questions that I believe every leader must ask themselves in the beginning stages of leadership at any level is "Who am I?" In essence, when you take the time to learn about yourself, you want to really dig deep and discover the characteristics and qualities that make you the unique person you are today. One of the primary reasons I believe this question is so vitally important to ask in the beginning stages of leadership is that when you know who you are, you discover the qualities and characteristics within that will enable you to obtain personal, career, and leadership success. In addition, when you discover who you are, you are able to reap many benefits that accompany self-awareness.

For example, when you know who you are, you can position yourself more effectively for leadership success, and you become more effective at surrounding yourself with the right people. You also make better decision in tough moments, you connect better with others, you have an easier time discovering your purpose in life, and, most importantly, you know what type of environment you must create for yourself in order to succeed personally and professionally as a leader. Leadership experts from the University of Stanford and Harvard University selected "knowing who you are" as the top leadership quality to develop in emerging leaders; both of these campus experts agreed in various articles that self-awareness was the number one quality to develop in emerging leaders. If you research the word *self-awareness*, you will find that this quality is about knowing who you are, knowing how to relate to the world, and having the ability to look at and discern inner thoughts, feelings, makeup, and beliefs about yourself, all of which are connected to the primary question "Who am I?" Experts on self-awareness will tell you that knowing who you are is key to your personal and leadership success at any level. They will encourage you to take the time to learn about who you are because many of the qualities you need in order to succeed in life as a leader are within. For example, as I will discuss later in this book, the strengths, passion, and vision you will need in order to succeed as a leader come from within. In addition, the personality that will help you succeed comes from within, the mindset of a champion that you will need comes from within, the intuitive voice that will help you succeed comes from within, and the purpose that you will need in order to reach your fullest potential as a leader comes from within as well. Ultimately, this means that if you are going to discover the key leadership qualities that are within you, you will have to ask yourself the question, "Who am I?"

This question has enabled me to become more effective as a leader, and it's one of the key leadership questions that has helped me create personal, career, and leadership success over the past ten plus years. The primary reason I feel so strongly about this statement is because of what happened when I discovered my strength to speak, my passion to impact lives through motivational speaking, and my ability to effectively follow my intuition and inner voice. I ended up developing a successful speaking business, I have improved my finances every year, I am living a full and joyous life, and, most importantly, I am serving others more effectively as a leader and making more of an impact in the world as a leader.

To help you discover who you are, I have provided you with four questions that will guide you in this process. I encourage you to think deeply about these questions and have conversations about self-awareness with trusted friends, family members, or mentors as well.

LEADERSHIP NOTES: _____

_____

_____

_____

_____

_____

_____

_____

_____

_____

_____

_____

_____

_____

_____

_____

_____

1

FOUR DISCUSSION QUESTIONS:
Do you possess self-awareness?

QUESTION ONE

If you could describe yourself with five specific words, how would you describe yourself? Please explain why you chose those specific words.

_____

_____

_____

QUESTION TWO

If others were given the opportunity to describe you to others with five specific words, how would they describe you? Please explain why you chose those specific words.

_____

_____

_____

QUESTION THREE

Based on your responses to the questions above, how would you best describe who you are as a leader and person?

_____

_____

_____

QUESTION FOUR

Based on what you have learned about yourself thus far, what type of leader do you envision yourself becoming, and what sort of organization is most conducive for your effectiveness as a leader?

_____

_____

_____

LEADERSHIP QUESTION #2
Do you possess the character to succeed as a leader?

A couple of years ago, I was doing extensive research on successful business leaders. During the research process, I came across an engaging article on effective leadership and read a powerful quote by Howard Schultz, former chairman and chief executive officer of Starbucks, who said, "Without character, nothing else matters." According to this highly successful leader, without character, it was almost impossible for any individual to succeed as a leader. When I first read this statement, I had some skepticism, but after thinking more deeply about character development as it relates to leadership, I ended up agreeing with Mr. Schultz that it is impossible to succeed as a leader without character. The primary reason I agree with his assertion is that history reveals to us that most people choose to follow leaders because of their character. Ultimately, if a person's character is tainted, every other aspect of their experience as a leader will eventually be tainted by this negative character attribute.

Great examples of this concept are common in the world of sports. For those of you who love sports, you can probably think of someone who had great talent in their area of expertise within the sports arena, but due to bad character, their success in the sports arena was immensely affected. In addition to the impact of bad character on the court or in the field, these talented and gifted men and women are often impacted off the court or field as well because of their lack of character. The same is true in the other arenas, including business, politics, and religion. Gifted, passionate, competent, and powerful leaders who are influencing people and doing great things for their organizations, community, and nation undergo tremendous destruction within their leadership experience because of their lack of character. These examples all point to the fact that if you are going to be an effective leader who makes a significant impact in the world, you must develop exceptional character.

Most people define exceptional character as having integrity; being honest, compassionate, trustworthy, loyal, fair, responsible, and ethical; treating all people with respect; and possessing a strong moral foundation. There is one more aspect of exceptional character that I believe is vitally important for emerging leaders to understand as well. This additional aspect of character was taught to me a few years ago by Dr. Henry Cloud, a bestselling author, psychologist, and international speaker, who said, "Exceptional character is exemplified by a leader when he has an ability to meet the demands of reality." This is not only about being morally and ethically right—it's about being able to act well under pressure, perform well in your area of expertise as a leader, and meet the tasks and demands of the people in your leadership position.

Let's say you want to become the president of a Fortune 500 company. Not only will exceptional character be exemplified in your ethical and morally right choices on the job, but your character will also be defined by how well you deal with challenges within your company or organization, how well you perform at your job, and how effective you are at meeting the tasks and demands of the people within your company or organization.

In effect, as leader of any organization or company, if you are going to develop exceptional character as a leader in that area of expertise, you must focus your efforts on evolving into a morally and ethical leader who becomes aware of the specific skills required to exemplify exceptional character in your area of expertise by developing into a leader who has the capacity to meet the tasks and demands of the people in an excellent manner.

To help you develop exceptional character as a leader in your area of expertise, I have provided you with four questions that will guide you in this process. I encourage you to think deeply about these questions and have conversations about your character with trusted friends, family members, or mentors as well.

LEADERSHIP NOTES: _____

_____

_____

_____

_____

_____

_____

_____

_____

_____

_____

_____

_____

_____

_____

_____

2

FOUR DISCUSSION QUESTIONS:
Do you possess the character to succeed as a leader?

QUESTION ONE

How would you describe a moral and ethical leader within your professional area of expertise?

_____

_____

_____

QUESTION TWO

On a scale of 1–10, how would you honestly rate yourself with regard to the moral and ethical leader you described above?

_____

_____

_____

QUESTION THREE

Over the next six months, which aspects of this type of leader that you described above do you need to work on the most?

_____

_____

_____

QUESTION FOUR

In addition to the leadership qualities listed above, what other characteristics of leadership must you develop over the next six months to a year in order to effectively meet the tasks and demands of the people you serve as a leader in an excellent manner in your desired area of expertise?

_____

_____

_____

LEADERSHIP QUESTION #3
Do you know your passion?

Throughout my life, I have gained a great deal of leadership insight and wisdom from a variety of people, but one of the most significant lessons I ever learned about leadership came from my friend Mikki Woodard, who said, "Every great leader has a story to tell because every great leader will be required to overcome a unique challenge or obstacle at some point in their leadership journey." In essence, regardless of how prepared you are to lead, at some point you will be required to deal with a challenging circumstance or situation as a leader. Although you will be able to use many strategies to overcome this unique challenge or circumstance, one foundational characteristic of leadership that will enable you to conquer different negative situations that could stop you from succeeding as a leader is a strong passion for the vision, cause, idea, company, or organization that you have the opportunity to lead.

This insight was revealed to me several years ago when I had the opportunity to watch an online interviewer ask Steve Jobs and Bill Gates the question "What is the key to success?" In a two-minute response, Mr. Jobs said, "You need to have a lot of passion for what you do because it's hard to succeed, and if you do not love what you are doing, there is a good chance that you are going to quit. But, if you have an extreme passion for something, the passion that comes from within will enable you to overcome the different challenges you will face." After hearing this powerful statement, I realized that if I was going to lead anything worthwhile, I had to make sure I was passionate about it because my passion for my vision, idea, cause, company, or organization would be the internal fuel that would enable me to overcome the numerous challenges that I could expect to face in my leadership journey.

Most people who study leadership and success understand the power of passion and the importance of having passion as a leader, but many of these people often encounter the question "How do I find my passion?" In essence, the question is: How do people find that intense emotion on the inside that makes them enthusiastic about a particular vision, cause, idea, company, or organization? Although there are many unique ways for individuals to discover their passion, the simplest way to help someone discover their passion is to challenge them to answer a series of questions such as the following: "What inspires you to act?" "What motivates you to help others?" "What captures your attention?" "What do you care deeply about" and "What are you willing to give 110% to?" Once questions like these are answered honestly by men and women who aspire to discover their passion in life, at some point in the leadership journey these individuals will figure out their passion in life. Once this transformational experience takes place, these individuals can expect more success as a leader, and this passion from within will enable these leaders to overcome every challenge, obstacle, or situation that tries to stop them from seeing their vision, dream, idea, or aspiration become a reality.

One of the greatest examples of this concept occurred in the life of a young man from Rochester, New York, who had the dream of playing on the high school basketball team. In this true story, the young man had autism, was considered too short to play basketball, was cut from the basketball team during his sophomore year, and had to serve as the manager of the team for two full years. Through all the challenges and obstacles, this young man continued to practice and envision himself playing on the basketball team one day. He finally got a chance to play in the last home game of the year because of his hard work and passion for the game. When he entered the game with four minutes left, he went six for eight from the field, scored approximately twenty points in the game, and had the most points of any player in that particular game.

Following this amazing event, Jason McElwain was recognized by Magic Johnson, the president of the United States of America, and many other influential leaders because of his ability to inspire and impact the lives of millions through perseverance, determination, and an inner passion to succeed in basketball. I recommend watching this inspirational story online. One of the biggest lessons we can all learn from the life of Jason McElwain is that if you have enough passion on the inside for a vision, dream, or goal, nothing can stop you from seeing that vision, dream, or goal become a reality. But to obtain the degree of passion that he had for basketball, you need to take time to discover the passion that lies within you and within every great and impactful leader.

To help you discover that inner passion, I have provided you with four questions to ask yourself, answer, and have conversations about with your trusted friends, family members, or mentors.

LEADERSHIP NOTES: _____

_____

_____

_____

_____

_____

_____

_____

_____

_____

_____

_____

_____

_____

_____

_____

3

FOUR DISCUSSION QUESTIONS:
Do you know your passion?

QUESTION ONE

What types of things do you care deeply about in life?

_____

_____

_____

QUESTION TWO

What types of things inspire you to act and help others?

_____

_____

_____

QUESTION THREE

What types of things do you love to do as a leader?

_____

_____

_____

QUESTION FOUR

Based on the questions above, what type of organization, company, or worthy cause do you believe would benefit from your passion as a leader?

_____

_____

_____

LEADERSHIP QUESTION #4
What core values do you live by?

Dr. Harry M. Jansen Kraemer Jr., a professor, author, and leadership expert at Northwestern University, once said in a *Forbes Magazine* article, "Leadership is about being rooted in who you are and what matters most to you." In essence, according to Dr. Kraemer, who is an expert on values-based leadership, leadership is about discovering your values in life and being true to the values that matter to you most. One of the primary reasons Dr. Kraemer and many other leadership experts believe that it is vitally important to discover your values and be true to those values as a leader is that when you lead with your values, you stay true to who you are. In addition, people who work with you have an easier time trusting you, your decision making becomes easier, you become more of an authentic leader, your strategic planning becomes easier, and you are able to set a standard for yourself as a leader that can enable you to experience greater performance and make a stronger impact within your sphere of influence.

In a powerful article written by Katherine Dean, Senior Vice President of the Wealth Planning Center within Wells Fargo's Wealth Management Group, Ms. Dean stated that values not only help you manage people effectively, but they also help you recruit the right people for your team. The primary reason values help leaders manage and recruit the right people for their team is that leaders who lead with their values can create shared values with the members of their team that lead to collective success. And, when a leader is able to develop shared values with the members of his or her team, he or she has the power to become more effective at inspiring and uniting different groups of people to do amazing things together as a team. This is why so many leadership experts encourage companies, organizations, and e-boards to create shared values among their teams—because when a leader is able to develop shared values with the members of his or her team, the people become more united, inspired, and focused on the vision or purpose of the organization.

Consequently, if you are going to lead with your values, it is extremely important that you understand what a value is, and it's also vitally important that you take the time to identify and develop the top ten values that you believe in as a leader of your organization, company, team, or e-board. According to various experts on this subject matter, values are described as ideas, beliefs, and philosophies that affect our behavior, decision making, and actions in life. Some specific examples of values that various leaders have created for themselves are integrity, ethical decision making, respect for everyone, honesty, excellence, service, personal responsibility, loyalty, work-life balance, family, love, innovation, commitment, and doing good to others. Although there are also other important values that have been identified by various leadership experts, these are a nice set of values that can help you begin to consider and develop the values that matter most to you and that you plan to live by as a leader in the twenty-first century.

To help you develop your values as a leader, I have provided you with four questions that will guide you in this process. I encourage you think deeply about these questions and have conversations about these values with trusted friends, family members, or mentors as well.

4

FOUR DISCUSSION QUESTIONS:
What core values do you live by?

QUESTION ONE
What are ten values that you live by right now as a leader?

_____

_____

_____

QUESTION TWO
Based on the ten values listed above, what are the top five values that you live by as a leader?

_____

_____

_____

QUESTION THREE
Based on the five values listed above, what are the top three values that you live by as a leader?

_____

_____

_____

QUESTION FOUR
Based on your top three values as a leader, what types of organizations, companies, or areas of expertise would benefit from having you as a leader?

_____

_____

_____

LEADERSHIP QUESTION #5
What are your core strengths as a leader?

Approximately fifteen years ago when I was a sophomore in college, I had a strong passion within to help people discover their vision in life. During this unique time in my life, I encouraged my friends to discover their personal strengths and talents. I realized at a young age that one of the keys to manifesting our vision or dreams in life as a leader is to discover and use the personal strengths and talents that we have been given. Unfortunately, during these power-coaching interactions with my fellow classmates in college, there were moments when people had a hard time discovering their strengths and talents because they had barriers and negative experiences that blocked them from seeing the strengths and talents within. Thankfully, after a couple of hours of coaching, these same people were able to finally discover the amazing strengths and talents they had been living with for years. Once these individuals discovered their strengths and talents, it became easier for them to discover their vision, and these men and women subsequently experienced greater personal, career, and leadership success because they were using their native strengths and talents to help them succeed in life.

About ten years later, I learned about a bestselling leadership book written by Marcus Buckingham entitled *Now, Discover Your Strengths*, which is geared toward helping people find, develop, and cultivate their strengths in order to do things they are gifted and talented at doing versus the opposite. Mr. Buckingham is so passionate about this philosophy because he believes that people who discover, focus, and use their strengths achieve greater success, increase performance, thrive in their professional area of expertise, experience more fulfillment in work, are more engaged and happy about life, and ultimately become better leaders. As the topic of strengths and leadership has become more popular, more people seem to be writing, talking, and sharing their opinions and research about the power of strengths-based leadership.

For example, in an article published in 2012 on the Gallup Blog by Jim Asplund, Chief Scientist, Strengths-Based Development and Performance Impact Consulting, this incredible expert talked about the important of strengths and shared seven specific reasons, based on his research, that we should all lead with our strengths. These included the fact that strength-based leaders who focus on their employees' strengths will likely see only 1% of their employees disengaged versus 22%. He also found that people who use their strengths every day are 6 times more likely to be engaged than those who do not. Mr. Asplund also discovered that when a team focuses on strengths, they have 12.5% greater productivity than a team that does not. And lastly, he found that teams receiving strengths feedback experience 8.9% greater profitability and 14.9% lower turnover rate.

Essentially, after learning about the power of discovering one's strengths and using them as a leader through my college experience and the work of Mr. Buckingham and Mr. Asplund, I began to notice that some of the greatest leaders our world has ever known became great because of their ability to discover, develop, cultivate, and use their strengths and talents as leaders. In addition, I also discovered in my personal life that when I function in my strengths, I experience more success in life, and knowing my strengths makes it easier to surround myself with the right people who would help me manifest the vision that I developed for myself as a national speaker, author, and leadership/diversity/relationship expert.

Like me and many other powerful and influential leaders of the past and present, if you are going to succeed as a leader and have an impact on the world, you must take the time to discover, develop, cultivate, and use your dominant strengths and talents in your area of expertise as a leader. To help you move effectively through this process, I encourage you to answer the four questions below to help you discover, develop, cultivate, and use your dominant strengths and talents as a leader.

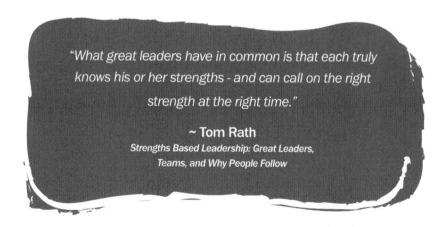

"What great leaders have in common is that each truly knows his or her strengths - and can call on the right strength at the right time."

~ Tom Rath
Strengths Based Leadership: Great Leaders, Teams, and Why People Follow

LEADERSHIP NOTES: _____

_____

_____

_____

_____

_____

_____

_____

_____

_____

_____

_____

_____

_____

_____

5

FOUR DISCUSSION QUESTIONS:
What are your core strengths as a leader?

QUESTION ONE
What are your top five strengths and talents?

_____

_____

_____

QUESTION TWO
What are your top five strengths and talents as a leader?

_____

_____

_____

QUESTION THREE
Have you taken the strengths-finder assessment by Marcus Buckingham? If not, visit **www.gallupstrengthscenter.com** and take the assessment. Then write down your strengths below.

_____

_____

_____

QUESTION FOUR
Based on the strengths that you have discovered about yourself, list some specific ways that you can begin leading others more effectively right now with your strengths.

_____

_____

_____

LEADERSHIP QUESTION #6
Do you have the mind of a great leader?

A few years ago, while I was visiting my family in Northern California, my grandmother asked me to attend an event with her and her friends to watch a popular movie entitled The Secret. Although I really did not feel like attending the event that night, I decided to go because it was my grandmother asking me to attend. Surprisingly, not only was the video extremely eye-opening for me, but the creators of this video did an amazing job of explaining the power and importance of positive thinking. The speakers and experts who were featured in the film did a phenomenal job of explaining the power that our thoughts can have on our personal, career, and leadership success.

Even though I had heard about the power of positive thinking for several years before attending this event with my grandmother, after watching the video, I was challenged to discipline my thought process as a leader, and I realized that many men and women fail to reach their greatest potential in life because they have not mastered their thought process. In effect, these are amazing people with huge amounts of potential to become great leaders in our world, but because these individuals have not mastered their thought process, they fail to reach their fullest potential as a leader. These potential leaders who have not mastered their thought process continually think pessimistically, have a problem trusting others, allow negative situations to stop them from pursuing their goal or dream, consistently have a bad attitude, experience low self-esteem, always seem to point the finger and blame someone for something within their organization or company, and have a difficult time reaching their fullest potential because of the negative and destructive mental road blocks within.

In contrast, the men and women who have learned how to master their thought process evolve into amazing leaders who attain greater levels of success, become more effective at communicating and impacting the members of their team, and usually make more of an impact in their community, nation, and world than those who have not mastered their thought process. One example of this concept is Thomas Edison. Thomas Edison not only created the light bulb, but he had to be so optimistic in his thinking that he could overcome 50,000 failed experiments before he actually created the vision that he discovered from within. Another example is President Barack Obama. Before President Obama became the first African American president in the history of the United States of America, he had to possess an attitude that was optimistic enough to overcome the unique challenges and negative opinions of others that manifested in his life because of the fact that America had never before elected an African American president. And lastly, when the Boston Red Sox were down 3-0 in the American League Championship Series to the New York Yankees in 2004, in order to make history and overcome the 3-0 deficit, they had to create an optimistic mindset about their chances of winning the series and doing something that more than 90% of teams have never been able to do. History was made in each of these three situations because these individuals were able to create the proper mindset that amazing leaders and champions must possess in order to accomplish great things.

Essentially, what we can learn from these amazing stories is that, as leaders in the twenty-first century, if we are going to master our thought process, it is important that we discipline ourselves to think positively and possess a great attitude at all times, and it's imperative that we have an ability to identify the negative realities in certain situations and develop positive and practical solutions to those problems. In effect, a positive-thinking leader must not only think positively, visualize positive things manifesting in his or her life, and have a great attitude at all times, but he or she must also be able to see and create something positive in the negative circumstances that every leader will face in their leadership journey. For instance, if something is causing you to have a bad attitude, as a leader you want to address the problem and optimistically develop a practical solution that you believe can change your negative mindset into a positive one.

To help you master your thought process, I have created a series of four questions that will help you improve your thought process. I encourage you to discuss these questions as well as your answers with your family, friends, and colleagues.

LEADERSHIP NOTES: _____

_____

_____

_____

_____

_____

_____

_____

_____

_____

_____

_____

_____

_____

_____

_____

_____

FOUR DISCUSSION QUESTIONS:
Do you have the mind of a great leader?

QUESTION ONE

If you became more optimistic and positive as a leader, how do you believe it would positively impact your leadership experience?

_____

_____

_____

QUESTION TWO

What roadblocks, experiences, or negative situations have affected your ability to keep a positive mindset and attitude about everything as a leader?

_____

_____

_____

QUESTION THREE

On a scale of 1–10, how optimistic are you as a leader in most situations?

_____

_____

_____

QUESTION FOUR

What specific steps can you begin doing today in order to discipline yourself to become more optimistic and positive as a leader?

_____

_____

_____

LEADERSHIP QUESTION #7
Do you have phenomenal intuitive intelligence?

Approximately twelve years ago, our campus organization invited the president of the university at the time to serve as a keynote speaker for one of our leadership events. The president agreed to speak at our event and delivered an insightful and eye-opening keynote presentation for the students within our organization. Although the entire presentation was filled with wisdom relevant to our group of leaders, the most powerful moment of the entire presentation occurred for me when the president stated that his greatest leadership attribute was being able to follow his gut. He explained several other key attributes of leadership, but the attribute that was most important to him as a leader was following his intuition.

In addition to sharing us with this vitally important leadership attribute, he also shared a powerful story about the evolution of this leadership skill set in his life before he became the president of our university. The story he used to illustrate this point took place while he served as president at the University of Nevada, Las Vegas. During that time, the university basketball team was playing an important game in Thomas Mack Arena with thousands of people cheering on their team. Suddenly, in the middle of the game, the president of our university shared that he received a random call from someone stating that they had planted a bomb in the arena and were threatening to set it off. The president had dealt with this type of event before, but at that moment he had to decide whether to stop the game and have everyone clear out of the building or disregard the call and allow the game to continue. Surprisingly, he decided to keep the game going because in his gut he felt that the bomb scare was a hoax. Thankfully for the entire university, he was correct!

After reflecting upon this leadership skill set for quite a few years, I recently came across a study related to this form of leadership. According to a study of 13,000 business executives conducted by Jagdish Parikh of Harvard University, 80% of these business executives attributed their success to relying on their intuition. Similarly, a senior executive at Shell Oil Company concluded that intuitive strategies are often found at the highest level of leadership within most organizations. And, Dr. Maidique stated that intuition played a huge role in 85% of the 36 major chief executive officers of major companies. Ultimately, what we can learn from these studies and the experience of my former university president is that intuitive intelligence is a key leadership skill set that every leader must acquire and develop in order to obtain personal, career, and leadership success.

Now, although there are many definitions of intuition, the one I like best is "an ability to look within and obtain direct knowledge without evident rational thought." In essence, intuition is a gut feeling, an internal instinct, a sixth sense, an inner voice, a spiritual faculty that does not explain but points the way, or an ability to reason or analyze a situation without really knowing about the situation. Some additional reasons that this leadership skill set is so important for leaders to possess in the twenty-first century is that your intuition will help you make effective decisions in uncertain situations, will reveal things to you about a person before you ever really get to know the person, can serve as protection from negative situations in certain situations, and, most importantly, can enhance your leadership capability and success at any level.

Unfortunately, this particular leadership skill set is rarely developed or built by emerging leaders because it's rarely talked about in leadership circles. However, once you learn about it, it's important to begin studying and learning how to develop this powerful leadership skill set that lies within each of us. Although this critical leadership skill will not develop overnight, if you work at developing it over time, it will become an extremely valuable resource for your personal, career, and leadership success.

To help you develop your intuitive intelligence, I have created a series of four questions that will help you improve this aspect of your leadership capacity. I encourage you to discuss these questions as well as your answers with your family, friends, and colleagues.

LEADERSHIP NOTES: _____

_____

_____

_____

_____

_____

_____

_____

_____

_____

_____

_____

_____

_____

_____

_____

_____

7

FOUR DISCUSSION QUESTIONS:
Do you have phenomenal intuitive intelligence?

QUESTION ONE

Are you aware of your intuition?

_____

_____

_____

QUESTION TWO

On a scale of 1–10, how effective are you at listening to your intuition in various circumstances as a leader? Please explain why you selected the answer that you chose.

_____

_____

_____

QUESTION THREE

On a scale of 1–10, how effective are you at following your intuition in certain situations as a leader? Please explain why you selected the answer that you chose.

_____

_____

_____

QUESTION FOUR

What specific adjustments do you plan to make in the next six months to a year in order to become more effective at developing and leading with your intuition?

_____

_____

_____

LEADERSHIP QUESTION #8
Are you a courageous leader?

Aristotle once said, "Courage is the virtue of all virtues." As a leader, I truly believe that without courage, you cannot become an effective leader because courage is the inner virtue that enables us to step up as a leader regardless of the danger, pain, rejection, failure, or challenges that stand between us making an impact in our community, nation, and world. The primary reason I feel so strongly about this concept is that you can have all the leadership qualities in the world, but if you never have the courage to act as a leader, nothing will happen because the courage to act ignites everything else to take shape in our lives as leaders.

An example of this leadership attribute transpired in my life in 2010. In late December of that year, I was flying back to Los Angeles, California, from an impactful leadership conference in Jacksonville, Florida. During that trip, I'd met many amazing people, and I'd received a clear vision of a national leadership conference that I wanted to create in Los Angeles entitled "The Circle of Change Leadership Conference." At the time, this was a new type of leadership conference that required a business plan, advisory board, executive team, and financial resources to fund a conference of this magnitude. Sadly for me at the time, I had none of the above. But, instead of sitting on my butt and waiting for the perfect time to make this conference a reality, I had the courage to act upon the vision from within and start taking the necessary steps to create this huge leadership conference without any viable resources.

As I began this courageous journey of making my vision a reality, I made a great deal of progress in the early stages, but I also faced many challenges, rejections, disappointments, and failures, which challenged the courageous leader within. Thankfully, though, after eleven months of pursuing my vision with all the courage that was within me, not only did I see the conference miraculously become a reality, but I also developed a leadership team, found sponsors for the event, and have seen hundreds of student leaders positively impacted over the past three years because I courageously acted upon the vision that I discovered within. Amid all the lessons that I was able to learn during this particular leadership journey, the most powerful lesson was that one first courageous step of faith in any given situation to make the world a better place as a leader can create a ripple effect that inspires, motivates, and empowers people and causes people and things to begin moving in our direction to help us manifest the visions and dreams that we possess as leaders in the twenty-first century. Without courage, these amazing experiences never happen for emerging or seasoned leaders, and people are not positively impacted around the world.

Now, although courage has been a vital characteristic of leadership for many years, over the past few years I have heard more leadership experts than ever before talk about the importance of courageous leadership. According to some of these experts, courageous leadership is about stepping up to the plate and taking action as a leader regardless of the situation or circumstance. In essence, regardless of how tough or difficult it may seem to be to make a certain decision as a leader, courageous leaders act upon the situation or circumstance. A recent article by Rod Edmonson that I read online discussed seven keys of courageous leadership that he believed every courageous leader must possess. Some of the specific leadership attributes discussed by Mr. Edmonson in the article included that courageous leaders do not bail on their team when things get tough, they are not afraid to make big request of others, they are willing to make the first move into uncharted territory, and they move by faith when the outcome is unclear. In addition to these characteristics of courageous leadership, leaders who possess courage are willing to make hard decisions regarding people who are no longer a good fit for them, they protect the vision of the group or organization in the face of criticism, hard economic times, and setbacks, and they are willing to implement needed changes when they are uncomfortable or not immediately popular.

To help you develop into a courageous leader of the twenty-first century, I have listed four questions for you to answer and discuss with friends, colleagues, and family members.

LEADERSHIP NOTES: _____

_____

_____

_____

_____

_____

_____

_____

_____

_____

_____

_____

_____

_____

_____

_____

_____

8

FOUR DISCUSSION QUESTIONS:
Are you a courageous leader?

QUESTION ONE

On a scale of 1–10, based on the description of a courageous leader, how courageous of a leader would you consider yourself? Please explain why you selected the answer that you chose.

_____

_____

_____

QUESTION TWO

Are there any specific things are holding you back from becoming more courageous as a leader in the twenty-first century?

_____

_____

_____

QUESTION THREE

What specific things can you do in order to become more courageous as a leader within your company or organization?

_____

_____

_____

QUESTION FOUR

What specific adjustments do you plan to make in the next six months to a year to become more courageous as a leader of your organization or company?

_____

_____

_____

LEADERSHIP QUESTION #9
Are you a purpose-driven leader?

During my years as a motivational speaker, one of the most common questions I have heard is, "How would you define success?" That question is really asking how I make the determination of whether or not someone has obtained success. Although success can look quite different to different people, I like to define success as making a difference in others' lives while also living a life of fullness and personal fulfillment through the manifestation of one's purpose on earth. The primary reason I have created this definition of success is that accomplishments are great, but if you are not impacting lives and experiencing personal fulfillment, I do not believe you are really succeeding or truly manifesting your purpose on earth to your full capacities.

I believe that leaders who obtain high levels of success are able to do so because they are purpose-driven leaders. In essence, these leaders of various organizations, companies, and groups are effective because they are able to discover, develop, and create a purpose that is bigger than them, brings them personal fulfillment, adds value to others, and makes the world a better place. Some of the primary reasons I believe it's so important to be a purpose-driven leader in the twenty-first century are that purpose-driven leaders are individuals who care more about the fulfillment of a mission than personal accomplishment, they care about the well-being of others, they are interested in impacting the lives of others, they have a meaningful reason behind their actions, they care about things that are bigger than themselves, and their drive on the inside as a purpose-driven leader inspires, motivates, and empowers the people around them to reach their fullest potential.

The term *purpose-driven leadership* is not new—it is a leadership characteristic that other leadership experts have discussed and written about, and have discovered works for leaders of various companies and organizations. For instance, in Jim Collins' book entitled Built to Last, he reported that leaders who led purpose- and values-driven organizations outperformed the general market and comparison companies by 15:1 and 6:1 respectively. In Corporate Culture and Performance by Harvard professors John Kotter and James Heskett, they reported that leaders of firms that shared purpose-driven, values-based cultures enjoyed 400% higher revenue and 700% greater job performance growth compared to other companies in similar industries. And lastly, an article on purpose-driven leadership by Dr. Maynard Brusman revealed that most individuals who follow leaders in various organizations and companies strive to be engaged in meaningful work that has a purpose behind it, are more engaged when there is a sense of higher purpose on the job, and value the work of an organization or company more when there is a mission or purpose statement. Ultimately, what we can learn from these different studies and articles is that purpose-driven leadership makes a difference in the lives of people around us, and it also has the power to have a direct positive effect on the performance of our company, organization, or team.

As emerging and seasoned leaders of the twenty-first century, in order to experience the benefits of purpose-driven leadership, you must be able to effectively discover, develop, and communicate the core purpose of your actions as the leader of your organization or company. To do so,

I encourage leaders to develop a set of at least five to seven authentic and passionate reasons they have decided to serve as the leader of a particular organization or company. Once these passionate reasons are clearly identified, I challenge leaders to create a powerful mission or purpose statement that inspires, motivates, and connects the leader and individuals who are part of the organization or company.

A great example of this concept is Herb Kelleher, the creator of Southwest Airlines. Essentially, Mr. Kelleher created this highly successful airline company because he wanted to create a fun and accessible airline experience for customers. Therefore, once his authentic and passionate reasons for starting the company were established, he effectively discovered, developed, and communicated a purpose that consisted of making travel fun and accessible. Because of this unique purpose, Southwest Airlines has distinguished itself from other airlines, has done extremely well in performance, has fully engaged the members of its team, has received great reviews from customers, and has experienced the success that follows emerging and seasoned leaders who are able to evolve into purpose-driven leaders.

Like Mr. Kelleher, as future leaders of the twenty-first century, we must make sure we take the time to ask ourselves a series of questions that will help us establish a strong foundation for purpose-driven leadership because it really makes a difference. To help you develop into a purpose-driven leader of the twenty-first century, I have listed four questions for you to answer and discuss with friends, colleagues, and family members.

LEADERSHIP NOTES: _____

FOUR DISCUSSION QUESTIONS:
Are you a purpose-driven leader?

QUESTION ONE

Provide five to seven passionate and authentic reasons that you have decided to serve as a leader of your desired organization or company?

_____

_____

_____

QUESTION TWO

Provide five to seven passionate and authentic reasons that others should serve with you in your desired organization or company?

_____

_____

_____

QUESTION THREE

What are the top three things that must manifest within your company or organization in order for you to experience complete mission fulfillment?

_____

_____

_____

QUESTION FOUR

Based on your previous responses, develop a core purpose and mission statement that will inspire, motivate, and empower you and your team of people.

_____

_____

_____

LEADERSHIP QUESTION #10
Are you an authentic leader?

For the past decade, one of the most popular buzz phrases used by leadership experts has been *authentic leadership*. Although the characteristics used to define an authentic leader have varied in different leadership circles, the definition that I like best when it comes to authentic leadership is: An authentic leader is someone who acts in accordance with their values, preferences, and needs as opposed to acting falsely in a manner that is done to please others, obtain awards, and avoid punishment. In essence, authentic leadership is about keeping it real and not being a fake person, and it's about creating an honest, ethical, and practical leadership style that is consistent with your personality and core values. Some of the primary reasons this style of leadership is so vitally important to develop as a leader are that authentic leaders obtain greater trust from their followers, have more sustainable performance, develop better relationships with others, are more likely to have a greater impact on the organization or company than inauthentic leaders, and experience a higher degree of well-being and comfort in the workplace than others.

Although people have talked about authentic leadership for years, the leadership concept became more relevant to various leaders in 2003, when a professor from Harvard University by the name of Bill George published a powerful book on authentic leadership entitled *Authentic Leadership: Rediscovering the Secrets to Creating a Lasting Value*. In this amazing book, Mr. George provided a clear and concise picture of authentic leadership, and he provided individuals with five key attributes of authentic leaders. The five attributes that he discussed in his book were that authentic leaders demonstrate passion for their purpose, they practice their values consistently, they lead with their hearts as well as their heads, they establish meaningful relationships, and they have the self-discipline to get results.

For example, when leaders are authentic, they have a strong passion for the purpose they are pursuing as a leader. They not only develop a moral compass of values they believe in, but they stay true to those values and beliefs regardless of the situation or circumstance they are facing as a leader. These types of leaders also exemplify empathy for their team, they have compassion for the members of their organization or company, they have the courage to address challenging situations, and they care more about the well-being of others than themselves. And lastly, authentic leaders have the heart and desire to establish meaningful relationships with others, and they have discipline with regard to the principles of success that are required in order to become a great leader of any organization or company.

Even though leadership success will require you to adapt to different circumstances and situations, if you are going to reap the benefits of authentic leadership, you must develop into an authentic leader. In order to do so, you will have to discover who you are and be true to who you are individually and with others, and you must be dedicated to personal growth, be focused on developing long-lasting relationships with others, be transparent with others about your failures and mistakes, and have the courage to lead and live by the values and principles that you earnestly believe in as a leader. Ultimately, if you can develop yourself into this authentic leader, you will avoid the pitfalls of leadership that result from a lack of authenticity, you will most likely see greater results as a leader, and you will become more effective at influencing, leading, and developing others because of the power of authentic leadership.

To help you develop into an authentic leader of your organization or company, I have created a series of four questions for you to answer and discuss with your friends, mentors, and family members.

LEADERSHIP NOTES: _____

_____

_____

_____

_____

_____

_____

_____

_____

_____

_____

_____

_____

_____

_____

_____

_____

10

FOUR DISCUSSION QUESTIONS:
Are you an authentic leader?

QUESTION ONE

On a scale of 1–10, based on the description of an authentic leader described in this book, how much of authentic leader are you? Please explain why you selected the answer that you chose.

_____

_____

_____

QUESTION TWO

On a scale of 1–10, how consistent are you at staying true to your values as a leader of your organization or company? Please explain why you selected the answer that you chose.

_____

_____

_____

QUESTION THREE

On a scale of 1–10, how much do you care about the well-being of the members of your team? Please explain why you selected the answer that you chose.

_____

_____

_____

QUESTION FOUR

What specific adjustments do you plan to make in the next six months to a year in order to become more authentic as a leader of your organization or company?

_____

_____

_____

LEADERSHIP QUESTION #11
Are you an emotionally intelligent leader?

Over the past twenty years, there have been many amazing experts who have researched, written about, and discussed the importance of leaders possessing emotional intelligence. Although I did not hear much about this powerful leadership skill set twenty years ago *because of my age*, I began to learn about this leadership characteristic a few years ago after a close friend told me that individuals who have high emotional intelligence make $29,000 more per year than those who do not, and that this skill set is a great predictor of personal, career, and leadership success. In essence, according to my good friend, individuals who have high emotional intelligence are more likely to make more money and become more effective as leaders within their respective companies and organizations than those who do not possess this leadership skill set.

So, like most people who have a strong desire to obtain personal, career, and leadership success, after hearing about this leadership concept, I began to investigate emotional intelligence. During this investigation process, I learned that two of the leading researchers on emotional intelligence were Peter Salovey and John D. Mayer. These two experts define emotional intelligence as an ability to monitor one's own and others' feelings and emotions, to discriminate among them, and to use this information to guide one's thinking and actions. In essence, these two men believe that individuals who possess high emotional intelligence will not only be effective at managing and understanding their own emotions, but they will be effective at managing, understanding, and reacting to the emotions of others as well. Essentially, what this means for leaders is that when someone has a negative reaction to a decision made by the leader of an organization or company, instead of just reacting emotionally, the leader who has high emotional intelligence will evaluate the emotions involved in the situation and will respond with the most effective emotional response to the situation.

As an avid sports fan, I've noticed that one of the greatest examples of this leadership concept was modeled by Phil Jackson. Phil Jackson was not only one of the most amazing coaches ever, but he was an eleven-time world champion. One of the primary reasons I believe he modeled emotional intelligence so well as a coach is that he was a master at dealing with difficult players and being able to effectively respond to emotional problems and situations that manifested during intense, pressured, and impactful games. Moreover, about five years ago, I was watching an interview with Shaquille O'Neal about Phil Jackson. During the interview, Mr. O'Neal stated that Phil Jackson was more effective than some of his former coaches in the NBA because he was brilliant at responding to the emotions of his team and calming them down in high-pressure situations. In essence, when the emotions of players were high during important moments during the NBA season, instead of becoming anxious and worried, Phil Jackson would react confidently and calmly to each situation that presented itself during the championship runs. Because of his effective emotional response to his players during those tough moments, Mr. Jackson got more out of his players than other coaches, which no doubt contributed to his having won the most NBA championships of any coach in the history of the NBA.

Similar to Phil Jackson, others leaders have done very well in their areas of expertise because they have developed high emotional intelligence. Although some people believe that this leadership characteristic is innate, many experts believe you can actually develop this leadership skill set. In order to develop this leadership concept within yourself, you must be aware of the four branches of emotional intelligence that were proposed by Mr. Salovey and Mr. Mayer.

The first branch of emotional intelligence is perceiving emotions, which deals with being able to understand different emotions that are conveyed through nonverbal signals such as body language and facial expressions. The second branch of emotional intelligence is reasoning with emotions, which deals with being able to effectively react and respond to the different emotions that you may have perceived within yourself or in others. The third branch of emotional intelligence is understanding emotions, which deals with being able to discover the root cause of the negative emotion that may have manifested within your area of influence as a leader. And the final branch of emotional intelligence is managing emotions, which deals with learning how to manage the emotions of one's self and others. Ultimately, if you can perfect these four areas of emotional intelligence, there is a great likelihood that you will increase your effectiveness as a leader and become more effective at leading others within your company or organization.

To help you develop into a highly emotionally intelligent leader within your organization or company, I have created a series of four questions for you to answer, develop, and discuss with your friends, mentors, and family members.

LEADERSHIP NOTES: _____

_____

_____

_____

_____

_____

_____

_____

_____

_____

_____

_____

11

FOUR DISCUSSION QUESTIONS:
Are you an emotionally intelligent leader?

QUESTION ONE

On a scale of 1–10, how effective are you at noticing, acknowledging, and responsibly handling your emotions? Please explain why you selected the answer that you chose.

_____

_____

_____

QUESTION TWO

On a scale of 1–10, how effective are you at perceiving the emotions of others? Please explain why you selected the answer that you chose.

_____

_____

_____

QUESTION THREE

On a scale of 1¬–10, how effective are you at responding to the emotions of others? Please explain why you selected the answer that you chose.

_____

_____

_____

QUESTION FOUR

What specific adjustments do you plan to make in the next six months to a year to become more emotionally intelligent as a leader?

_____

_____

_____

CHAPTER TWO
THE OPERATIONAL LEADER

According to John Maxwell, one of the world's leading experts on leadership development, operational leaders provide stability to an organization, they have a knack and ability to create infrastructure that works to accomplish the needs of others in an organization, and they create systems that transform needs into solutions. In effect, the operational leader knows how to effectively produce positive results as the leader of an organization, company, or group of people within his or her sphere of influence.

In this second chapter, I have developed a set of eleven new questions that are specifically geared toward helping you evolve into an effective operational leader of your organization, company, or team of people. In this chapter, you will not only learn and reflect upon a series of questions that revolve around the characteristics of an operational leader, but you will also discover specific leadership skills that you must develop in order to effectively lead the members of your organization and evolve into one of the World's Next Top Leaders!

LEADERSHIP QUESTION #12
Do you have a vision?

Approximately seven years ago, I was asked to appear as a guest on a local television talk show to discuss the impact on the Millennial Generation of the incident that transpired in New York City on September 11, 2001. One of the main reasons the show's producers wanted me to appear as a guest on their show was that I was young and had written my first book a couple of years earlier, entitled *Vision, the Answer to Generations X and Y.* Although my goal for the local television talk show was to talk about the key points in my book that related to the incident that transpired in New York City, I was doing some personal research before the show and discovered a recurring trend. This recurring trend consisted of three words: rebuilding, restructuring, and redefining. In essence, over the five-year span following the devastating events in New York City on 9-11, not only was our country rebuilding, restructuring, or redefining certain monuments and other things in America, but the challenges we were facing as a nation moved us into a season of rebuilding, restructuring, and redefining in the early part of the new millennium as well.

For example, in 2001, because of the incidents that transpired in New York City on September 11, 2001, we were put in an uncomfortable situation of rebuilding the lives of families and buildings in New York City. In 2003, we went to war with Iraq, and one of the common themes that many people were hearing about from media outlets was rebuilding. In 2004, one of the popular slogans of the Kerry/Edwards presidential campaign was rebuilding a stronger America. In 2005, after the devastating events of Hurricane Katrina in New Orleans, our country was forced to restructure and rebuild the lives of families and monumental buildings in New Orleans. By 2006, our nation began to focus our attention on rebuilding the educational system because of the staggering dropout rates in high schools and restructuring immigration policies in this country because of the immigration challenges that were being presented by certain political parties and associations. The common theme that ran through these unique challenges that manifested in America from 2001–2006 continued from 2007–2013 as well, in issues including global warming, climate change, becoming greener in various aspects of our lives, change, innovation, and redefining marriage.

After discovering this common trend in America over such a long period of time, I saw the importance of vision more than ever in our nation. I firmly believe in my heart that the leaders of the future will be the men and women who are able to create fresh, new visions for the twenty-first century. They will be men and women who not only possess exceptional leadership skills but who also possess vision. One of the main reasons I feel so strongly about this is because the beginning stages of rebuilding, restructuring, or redefining anything start with a vision, which I define as the ultimate goal discovered from within to make a positive impact in your community, nation, or world.

Now, although you may not have a vision for some of these major issues and problems that are affecting our communities, nation, and world right now, if you are going to be an effective leader of anything, you must understand the key components that are required in order to develop an effective vision and also actually create a vision. Some of the primary reasons that it's essential to be able to create an effective vision as a leader are that your vision helps you inspire others, brings solutions to problems, gives your company and organization meaning and purpose, gives you and others around you hope in tough situations, gives you direction, and gives you a clear picture of your future. Most importantly, there has never been a great leader who has not been able to create an effective vision. In essence, when you think of all the great leaders of our past and present, you will find that they were able to obtain great personal, career, and leadership success because they had an ability to create an effective vision of the future that inspired and motivated the lives of others.

Even though there are many ways that a leader can create an effective vision, there are some key things that every leader must think about when creating a vision. Some of the key things to think about when you are creating your vision as a leader are: Is your vision original and unique? Is your vision connected to your gifting or strong core competency as an organization? Are you and your group inspired and passionate about the vision? Does your vision bring value to others? Is your vision clear, concise, captivating, and quantifiable? Does your vision give you direction? Is your vision something you would do for free? Does your vision impact the lives of others? And finally, does your vision inspire others to have a strong desire to help you make it a reality? These questions, along with many others, are important to ask yourself during this process of creating an effective vision for you and the members of your team.

Once you have created this effective vision as a leader, the next thing you want to do is write down the vision and place it somewhere that you and the members of your team can see it every day. In addition to writing down the vision for everyone to see daily, you also want to repeat it over and over to yourself and the members of your team every day so that the vision becomes ingrained in the minds of the people who are destined to help you make your vision a reality as a leader. Ultimately, once this is accomplished, you will begin to see the power that comes to a leader and group of people when they are able to create a powerful vision for their organization or company.

To help you develop or strengthen your vision, I have created a series of four questions for you to answer, develop, and discuss with your friends, mentors, and family members.

12

FOUR DISCUSSION QUESTIONS:
Do you have a vision?

QUESTION ONE

Do you have a vision? If not, take the time to answer the questions discussed in this part of the book to develop your vision as a leader. Then record your vision on the lines below.

_____

_____

_____

QUESTION TWO

Is your vision clear, concise, and captivating to others? In essence, is it clear to understand, no longer than one sentence, and inspiring to others?

_____

_____

_____

QUESTION THREE

Where do you plan to write down your vision so that you and the members of your team can see the vision every day?

_____

_____

_____

QUESTION FOUR

How do you plan to make sure that everyone within your organization or company is hearing about the vision daily and that you are ingraining it within their minds so that you are all on the same page?

_____

_____

_____

LEADERSHIP QUESTION #13
Do you have a strategic action plan?

When I was a senior in high school, my high school basketball coach would always tell our team, "If you fail to plan, you should plan to fail." One of the primary reasons my basketball coach felt so strongly about this statement is that he strongly believed that many people have the ability to reach their vision or dreams in life, but they fail to do so because they never take the time to develop a strategic plan of action. Consequently, many men and women are able to create big, audacious, and powerful dreams, but only a few of these men and women will see their vision or dream become a reality because most people fail to develop a strategic action plan. Thankfully, because of the lessons I learned from my former high school basketball coach, I have seen many visions and dreams manifest in my life because of my keen awareness and understanding of the importance of developing a strategic action plan directly after I have created a powerful vision for success.

According to a 2005 study done by ThinkTQ, a training and publishing organization, this has not always been the case in America. For example, in their study on strategic action planning, they discovered that only 26 percent of people focus on specific, tangible targets for what they want in life; only 19 percent of people set goals aligned with their purpose, mission, and passion; only 15 percent write down their goals with specific measurable results; only 12 percent maintain a clearly defined goal for every major interest and life role; only 12 percent identify related daily, weekly, and long-term goals with deadlines; and only an astonishingly low 7 percent take daily action toward the attainment of at least one goal per day. Ultimately, what these findings reveal to me is that one of the main reasons so many people are not reaching their fullest potential in life is probably a result of not taking the time to develop an effective strategic action plan.

Sadly, this lack of strategic action planning not only affects ordinary people, but it affects the success of leaders as well. In essence, when leaders fail to develop a strategic action plan, the entire organization or company they are responsible for can be severely affected as well. So, if you are going to be one of the World's Next Top Leaders, it's not only important for you to have a powerful vision that is clear, concise, and captivating, but it's also vitally important that you know how to develop an effective strategic action plan.

I define a strategic action plan as a set of short-term and long-term goals that enable you to reach your vision or dream. The primary reason I like to use this definition is that the ultimate purpose of the strategic action plan is to help you manifest the dream or vision you have created as a leader. Similar to the creation of an effective vision, in order to experience the power of a strategic action plan, there are some key things that every leader must consider as part of this planning process.

The first thing to consider in the strategic action planning process is your current and desired future outcome for the organization or company. In essence, you want to be fully aware of your present situation and fully clear about the place where you see yourself in the future. Secondly, to the best of your ability, you want to consider developing a set of goals that will help you move from your current situation to your future situation. This can take some time, but if you are diligent in this process, it will make such a difference for you long-term. Then thirdly, once you have developed this set of goals, you want to consider making sure that these short-term and long-term goals are SMART (Specific, Measurable, Attainable, Realistic, and Timely) daily, weekly, monthly, yearly, and long-term goals that will help you attain your vision or dream. These types of goals are great because they help you stay focused and realistic about the things you will need to do in order to see your strategic action plan work for you and see your vision become a reality. Essentially, when you have effectively listed your daily, weekly, monthly, yearly, and long-term SMART goals, you are now set to act on this strategic action plan and pursue your amazing vision as a leader. As you embark on this leadership journey with your vision and strategic action plan, it's critical that you be prepared for the challenges, adjustments, new strategies, and other unique things that will occur during this leadership journey.

To help you in this strategic action planning process, I have created a series of four questions for you to answer, develop, and discuss with your friends, mentors, and family members.

LEADERSHIP NOTES: _____

_____

_____

_____

_____

_____

_____

_____

_____

_____

_____

_____

_____

_____

_____

_____

_____

13

FOUR DISCUSSION QUESTIONS:
Do you have a strategic action plan?

QUESTION ONE

Do you have a strategic action plan? If not, take some time to develop a quick strategic plan of action for how you plan to make your vision a reality.

_____

_____

_____

QUESTION TWO

As part of your strategic action plan, what are five short-term and long-term goals that you plan to execute in order to see your vision become a reality?

_____

_____

_____

QUESTION THREE

Are your short-term and long-term goals SMART (Specific, Measurable, Attainable, Realistic, and Timely) goals?

_____

_____

_____

QUESTION FOUR

Are you prepared for the challenges, adjustments, and new strategies that may be required in order to execute your strategic action plan and see your vision become a reality?

_____

_____

_____

LEADERSHIP QUESTION #14
Do you have a dream team?

A couple of years ago, I was visiting one of my best friends in Denver, Colorado. During this short vacation, my friend had a small get-together with some close friends in the area. One of the close friends who attended the event had just been named executive of the year of a major Fortune 500 company. As you might imagine, I started to ask her a variety of questions about the keys to her success with this major company. Shockingly, instead of providing me with her five secrets to corporate success, she told me to look at my hand. So, I looked at my hand and confusingly asked her why she wanted me to look at my hand. After five minutes of discussion about my hand, she finally told me that the reason she wanted me to look at my hand is that my hand represents the five closest people in my life, and the five closest people in her life had a direct impact on her success in the company. Now, these five people were not just any people—they were strategically selected by this executive early in her career, and because of her wise selection, she experienced great success in her career as a leader.

Similar to this executive of the year, if you are going to obtain personal, career, and leadership success in the twenty-first century, not only do you have to surround yourself with the right people, but you must actually create a dream team. The coined term *dream team* was created by a good friend of mine named Valerie Rowe, and the reason it's called a dream team is because it's a group of important people who support and help you manifest your dream or vision. It's important for leaders to develop a DREAM TEAM because the people on your DREAM TEAM provide you with the encouragement and inspiration needed in tough situations, they give you great ideas and wisdom in challenging circumstances, and they help you attain your vision or dream faster than you would without them. Also, they teach you lessons you may never have learned without them, and most importantly, without a DREAM TEAM, you will never be able to reach your fullest potential as a leader because every great leader needs amazing people around them.

Now, although you can add anyone you see fit to your DREAM TEAM, there are certain people whom I believe every leader should include in this special group. The first type of person that every leader should include in their DREAM TEAM is a mentor. I consider a mentor to be someone I can learn from, someone I can gain insightful wisdom from, someone I can be accountable to, and, most importantly, someone who has successfully done what I desire to do as a leader in the future. The second type of person that every leader should include in their DREAM TEAM is a peer-mentor. A peer mentor is someone who is not more experienced than me but is pursuing the same things as me, desires the same type of success in life as a leader as me, and can provide me with the same sort of benefits that I can obtain from my mentor. The third type of person I believe every leader should include in their DREAM TEAM is your romantic partner. This person should be included in your DREAM TEAM because they will know you the best, be with you the most, and probably have one of the greatest impacts on your life. The fourth type of person that every leader should include in their DREAM TEAM is a best friend or family member. Similar to the relationship partner, I believe this person is vitally important to have on your DREAM TEAM because most people are close to their family or friends, most people consistently look to their family or friends for advice, and most of your family or friends will desire for you to succeed and will not be afraid to be honest with you in tough situations. And lastly, the fifth type of person you should include in your DREAM TEAM is a mentee. A mentee is someone you empower, encourage, enhance, and make better. Although some people may not see growth with this type of relationship, I have found that having a mentee in your life can be one of the most beneficial and powerful relationships you will ever have because you will learn a great deal from each other.

Once you have determined the types of people you plan to add to your DREAM TEAM, the final thing to consider is, does your DREAM TEAM of amazing people enhance your life as a leader, do they encourage you, do they make you better, do they inspire you, do they tell you the truth, do they support you in the good and bad times, do they love you, do they believe in you, do they want the best for you, do they enlighten you, do they teach you new things, and most importantly, are they committed to supporting and helping you make your dream or vision a reality? Ultimately, if this amazing group of people does support you and want to help you attain your vision or dream, I have no doubt within my mind that you and the members of your DREAM TEAM will do some amazing things together within your community, nation, or world as leaders of the twenty-first century.

To help you develop this awesome DREAM TEAM, I have created a series of four questions for you to answer, develop, and discuss with your friends, mentors, and family members.

LEADERSHIP NOTES: _____

_____

_____

_____

_____

_____

_____

_____

_____

_____

_____

_____

14

FOUR DISCUSSION QUESTIONS:
Do you have a dream team?

QUESTION ONE

Do you have a DREAM TEAM? If you do not have a DREAM TEAM, take this time to reflect and think about the five people you would like to be part of your DREAM TEAM.

_____

_____

_____

QUESTION TWO

Does your DREAM TEAM include a mentor, peer mentor, family member, friend or significant other, and mentee? If not, think about some people who could serve as a mentor, peer mentor, family member, friend or significant other, and mentee.

_____

_____

_____

QUESTION THREE

In addition to your five core people, who are some other individuals you could add to your DREAM TEAM?

_____

_____

_____

QUESTION FOUR

Do these members of your DREAM TEAM have a strong desire to help and support you in making your vision or dream a reality?

_____

_____

_____

LEADERSHIP QUESTION #15
Are you a solution-focused leader?

Throughout my young-adult life, I have learned many amazing lessons from my pastor, Bishop Clarence E. McClendon. One of the most impactful leadership moments for me came several years ago when he said, "If you want to be a great leader, you must be a great servant and exceptional problem solver." In essence, according to my pastor, one of the characteristics of an exceptional leader is the strong ability to serve others in an excellent manner and effectively develop solutions to some of the most challenging problems. One of the main reasons I believe my pastor felt so strongly about this statement is that he had discovered that individuals who are given the opportunity to serve as presidents, CEOs, and executives of major organizations and companies are not only required to serve more people, but they are asked to solve the problems that others are not able to solve within their respective organization or company.

Just a few months after I heard this powerful statement from my pastor, I watched a well-known journalist interview President Obama. During this powerful discussion, the president said, "If a problem gets to me, it probably got to me because it was a problem that could not be solved by others." In essence, the president revealed in this interview that great leaders obtain greatness because they are able to develop effective solutions to problems that others cannot solve. Ultimately, this piece of wisdom taught me that if I was going to be an effective leader in the twenty-first century, I would need to be a solution-focused leader.

Although some have defined solution-focused leadership as a culture of motivation that focuses on what is working and how to do more of it, I like to define a solution-focused leader as someone who makes the decision to focus their efforts on developing solutions to various problems within the organization or company instead of pointing the finger, complaining, blaming others for the problem, and allowing negative situations to distract them from the purposed vision or goal within the organization or company. Solution-focused leaders focus their efforts on solutions to problems rather than treating others unfairly and allowing the problems to distract them from the vision of the organization or company. They are not afraid of challenging situations, they are not afraid of failure, they are willing to spend months and years developing multiple solutions to a problem until it is solved, and they fully believe that there is a solution to every problem. This type of leader becomes very attractive to major organizations and companies because they make others around them better, they reap huge benefits because of their ability to apply this style of leadership, and they have an enormous impact on the organization or company they are associated with. Because of this leadership perspective and attitude, these types of leaders enable people to perform better, develop solutions to problems that enhance an organization's effectiveness, and become irreplaceable because they have an ability to do things that others are not able to do as a leader. They impact the lives of millions because of the positive transformation that occurs when someone develops a solution to a problem.

To help you develop into a solution-focused leader, I have created a series of four questions for you to answer, develop, and discuss with your friends, mentors, and family members.

15

FOUR DISCUSSION QUESTIONS:
Are you a solution-focused leader?

QUESTION ONE

On a scale of 1–10, how effective are you at developing solutions to various challenges and problems? Please explain why you chose this answer.

_____

_____

_____

QUESTION TWO

Based on your response to the previous rating, what specific things must you do in order to evolve into a more effective solution-focused leader?

_____

_____

_____

QUESTION THREE

What specific things can you do on a daily basis to become more effective at developing solutions to some of the most challenging problems in the world?

_____

_____

_____

QUESTION FOUR

As the leader of your organization or company, what specific things can you do today in order to become more of a solution-focused leader within your organization or company?

_____

_____

_____

LEADERSHIP QUESTION #16
Are you an effective communicator?

When I think about successful leaders such as Dr. Martin Luther King Jr., Bill Clinton, Susan B. Anthony, John F. Kennedy, President Obama, Jack Welch, Winston Churchill, Malcolm X, Abraham Lincoln, and Mother Teresa, these leaders all had in common the ability to effectively communicate their message to others. Although each leader had a unique message for his or her specific task as a leader, they were all effective at communicating a message that inspired, motivated, and empowered others to act on the vision that was conveyed in their message. Like the leaders listed above, if you're going to be an effective leader of the twenty-first century, you must be an effective communicator whose message inspires, motivates, and empowers others to act on the vision you have created as a leader.

Although leaders must understand how to use different communication strategies for different settings and people within an organization or company, there are some common truths that will enable a leader to communicate to others more effectively. The first truth about effective communicators is that they understand, know, and listen to their audience and know how to effectively create a message that positively resonates with the people they are trying to reach. The second truth about amazing communicators is that they are effective at reaching others because they have an amazing ability to turn a complex message into something that is accessible and clearly understood by those who may not share their knowledge or background. In essence, they can take a complex problem and make it practical, relatable, and relevant to any particular audience.

The third truth about effective communicators is that they are effective with their audiences because they understand the enormous impact that their behaviors, actions, nonverbal communication, vocal tone, values, and personal experiences can have on a message communicated to others. The fourth truth about powerful communicators is that they all have the passion, charisma, optimism, and enthusiasm required to deliver a message that inspires, motivates, and empowers the lives of others. The fifth truth that effective communicators understand is that the setting of a communicated message can affect the effectiveness of the message and that the impact of a message occurs because the communicator has a powerful and clear purpose behind the message that is being conveyed. And lastly, the final truth that we can see in effective communicators is that they understand the impact that words, quotes, phrases, and statistics can have on a message in various circumstances and situations.

According to Richard Boyatzis, author of *The Competent Manager,* once you are able to develop the communication skills needed to effectively motivate, inspire, and empower the members of your organization, not only will you obtain greater results from the members of your organization or company, but you will become a more effective leader as well. One of the primary reasons Boyatzis is so confident about this truth is that he discovered in the early '80s that the most effective managers in his study of 253 people were very good communicators who were effective at verbal and nonverbal communication, giving persuasive presentations, communicating clearly to others, and motivating and gaining cooperation from others.

To help you develop into a more effective communicator, I have created a series of four questions for you to answer, develop, and discuss with your friends, mentors, and family members.

16

FOUR DISCUSSION QUESTIONS:
Are you an effective communicator?

QUESTION ONE

On a scale of 1–10, how effective are you as a communicator? Please explain why you chose this answer.

_____

_____

_____

QUESTION TWO

Based on your response to the previous rating, what specific things must you do in order to evolve into a better communicator as a leader?

_____

_____

_____

QUESTION THREE

What specific things can you do on a daily basis to become more effective at communicating with others?

_____

_____

_____

QUESTION FOUR

As the leader of your organization or company, what specific things can you do today in order to become more effective as a communicator within your organization or company?

_____

_____

_____

LEADERSHIP QUESTION #17
Are you a competent leader?

In the beginning stages of my speaking career, I always thought that my public speaking abilities would be the key to establishing a successful speaking career. Surprisingly, after a couple of months, I discovered that my public speaking skills were important, but if I was going to develop a successful speaking career, I had to develop quality business skills, effective marketing strategies, and a specific area of expertise that I would share with audiences all across the country. As a 24 year old, I was not much of an expert, marketing professional, or savvy businessman, but throughout my speaking career over the past eight years, I believe that I have experienced increasing success because I have focused my efforts as a national speaker on becoming an expert on leadership, diversity, and relationships. In essence, as a motivational speaker, not only have I taken the time to further develop my public speaking skills, but I have constantly worked on developing myself into a competent public speaking expert on the different topics that I share with audiences throughout the country. Similar to my own journey, if anyone is going to be an effective leader of the twenty-first century, they must focus their efforts on becoming an expert and competent leader in their area of expertise as well because this skill set is one of the requirements of great leadership within any professional arena.

One of the primary reasons I strongly believe that emerging leaders of the twenty-first century must be competent leaders is because a leader's competence can determine whether people respect or follow him or her. Being a competent leader is also important because effective leaders set an example for others, inspire others, develop and build others around them, normally know what they are doing, and build credibility and trust with others. Ultimately, what this means is that if you lack competence, you will probably struggle as a leader because it's almost impossible to serve as an effective leader of your organization or company if you lack competence in your area of expertise.

Although there are many words used to describe a competent leader, I like to define a competent leader as someone who knows how to do their job well as measured against the standard. In essence, a competent leader is someone who knows their area of expertise really well and knows how to get the job done in an excellent manner. This type of leader is also knowledgeable, experienced, and well qualified for the position of leadership. Moreover, when people see this leader in the workplace, they witness a leader who does not settle for mediocrity believes in excellence, strives to become better every day, goes the extra mile, has a strong work ethic, knows their job well, is an ongoing learner in their area of expertise, and does an amazing job at developing leaders around them.

For leaders who desire to develop into competent leaders, the first step is making a decision about the specific area of expertise that you desire to develop your competence in. Secondly, once you discover your area of expertise, you want to study your craft daily, gain experience in your area of expertise, find mentors who can teach you about your area of expertise, and strive to get better in this specific area every day.

Ultimately, after years of experience, training, and various lessons in your area of expertise, you will find yourself developing into an amazing, competent leader within your area of expertise. And when this happens, the impact you will have as a leader will be incredible!

To help you begin this development process as a competent leader, I have created a series of four questions for you to answer, develop, and discuss with your friends, mentors, and family members.

> "A competent leader can get efficient service from poor troops, while on the contrary an incapable leader can demoralize the best of troops."
>
> ~ John J. Pershing

LEADERSHIP NOTES: _____

_____

_____

_____

_____

_____

_____

_____

_____

_____

_____

_____

_____

_____

_____

_____

_____

_____

17

FOUR DISCUSSION QUESTIONS:
Do you have the mind of a great leader?

QUESTION ONE

As a leader, what specific competencies must you develop in order to become an expert in your preferred professional field of interest?

_____

_____

_____

QUESTION TWO

What specific things must you do in order to develop the specific competencies that are required of you in order to become an expert in your area of expertise?

_____

_____

_____

QUESTION THREE

What individuals would you consider experts in your desired area of expertise? What types of things can you do to learn from these individuals who have mastered their craft in your desired area of expertise?

_____

_____

_____

QUESTION FOUR

What specific things can you do daily in order to evolve into an expert in your desired area of expertise as a leader?

_____

_____

_____

LEADERSHIP QUESTION #18
Are you effective at using different leadership styles?

Several years ago, I was having a discussion with a good friend of mine who serves as the director of a career center in Southern California. As the director, it was her responsibility to manage and lead approximately ten people within her office. Shockingly to some, she discovered that because of the different personalities within her workplace environment, using one leadership style for all the members of her team did not work. So, instead of becoming frustrated with certain people who did not respond to her leadership style, she decided adjust her leadership style with each person who worked for her. Because of her ability to adjust her leadership style within the workplace environment, not only did she obtain amazing results as a leader, but everyone in the office cherished and loved her.

What we can learn from my friend is that if we are going to be effective at leading diverse groups of people in the twenty-first century, we must understand how to use different leadership styles with diverse types of people in various situations. One of the main reasons this leadership skill set is so important is that the twenty-first century workplace will be the most diverse workplace ever in world history, and in order to effectively lead diverse groups of people, emerging and seasoned leaders must know how to use different leadership styles with diverse groups of people. This skill set is also important because in order to effectively adjust your leadership style for difference situations as a leader, you must have an understanding of the diverse leadership styles that can be used in certain situations.

Throughout the years, there have been many different leadership styles developed by a diverse group of leadership experts. For example, in 1939, Kurt Lewin, a social psychologist, led a group of researchers to identify three different leadership styles: authoritarian leadership, participative leadership, and delegative leadership. Authoritarian leadership consisted of leaders telling their employees exactly what to do without any input from the employees. Participative leadership consisted of leaders including one or more employees in the decision-making process. And lastly, delegative leadership consisted of leaders allowing employees to make decisions on their own. Even though each leadership style has a specific purpose for different situations or scenarios, it's the leader's responsibility to determine which leadership style is most effective for the people they are leading within their respective organizations.

Now, although I strongly believe that each of the three leadership styles above can be used effectively in certain situations in the twenty-first century, personally, I believe that the two most important leadership styles for leaders to understand in the twenty-first century are participative leadership and transformational leadership. The primary reason I strongly believe that these two leadership styles are so important to understand is that these leadership styles fit the makeup of the twenty-first century culture and society and are considered by certain leadership experts to be the most effective leadership strategies to use in an ever-changing and economically uncertain business world. Ultimately, what this means is that with the constant changes and economic uncertainty that we see in the twenty-first century, every leader of the twenty-first century must understand how to effectively serve as a transformational and participative leader.

As I stated earlier, participative leadership is a leadership style that enables the members of the team to participate in the decision-making process of the group. This leadership style involves the leader letting others help in making the tough decisions for the group, organization, company, or team. According to James MacGregor Burns and Bernard M. Bass, transformational leadership is a form of leadership that occurs when a leader broadens and elevates the interests of his or her employees, generates awareness and acceptance of the purpose and mission of the team, and causes employees to look beyond their own self-interests to the good of the group. In effect, transformational leadership manifests when leaders commit themselves to providing the members of the team with the tools and resources to flourish while also believing that it's their responsibility to go beyond satisfying the current needs through rewards to moving followers toward achievement and growth. Both of these leadership styles involve constant communication, great compassion for one another, trust, a shared and collective vision or purpose, and a strong desire for everyone to succeed, which means that as the world's next top leaders, we must possess these different leadership characteristics.

To help you begin this development process with different leadership styles for diverse situations, I have created a series of four questions for you to answer, develop, and discuss with your friends, mentors, and family members.

LEADERSHIP NOTES: _____

_____

_____

_____

_____

_____

_____

_____

_____

_____

_____

_____

_____

_____

_____

_____

18

FOUR DISCUSSION QUESTIONS:
Are you effective at using different leadership styles?

QUESTION ONE

On a scale of 1–10, how effective are you at using different leadership styles in diverse situations? Please explain why you chose this answer.

_____

_____

_____

QUESTION TWO

Based on your response to the previous rating, what specific things must you do in order to become more effective at using different leadership styles for diverse situations?

_____

_____

_____

QUESTION THREE

What specific things can you do on a daily basis to become more effective at using these different leadership styles?

_____

_____

_____

QUESTION FOUR

As the leader of your organization or company, what specific things can you do today in order to become more effective at using these different leadership styles in diverse situations you encounter?

_____

_____

_____

LEADERSHIP QUESTION #19
Are you an ethical leader?

John Wooden, the former basketball coach and legend at the University of California, Los Angeles, once said, "Your talent will get you to the top, but it will take character to stay on top." In essence, according to Mr. Wooden, if you're talented enough in a specific area of expertise, you can emerge as a leader, but in order to maintain long-term success as a leader, you must have character and be an ethical leader. Although there are many definitions of an ethical leader, I like to define an ethical leader as someone who not only does the right thing but also leads and makes decisions based on values such as integrity, honesty, fairness, equality, justice, compassion, respect, and a desire for the common good of everyone involved. In effect, an ethical leader is someone who puts the good of the organization before their own interests; who treats everyone with fairness, honesty, and respect at all times; who leads with integrity and moral excellence; and who can be trusted to make the right decisions in tough circumstances and situations.

Some of the primary reasons it's important for leaders to be ethical are because ethical leadership improves your reputation with others, attracts strategic partners who can help you fulfill your vision as a leader, motivates people toward excellence and personal growth, and leads to successful organizations, companies, groups, and teams. Ethical leadership also enables the leader to build more trust and credibility with others and protects both the leader and the organization or company that the leader represents from challenges and problems that arise with unethical leadership. Ultimately, when a leader decides to become an ethical leader within their organization, company, group, or team, not only will this leader become more effective in their desired endeavors, but they will be able to create long-lasting relationships and sustainable success as well.

A great example of this concept is the Walt Disney Company. When you study the history of Disney, you learn that not only has their leadership valued positive ethics, but they have created an ethical code of conduct that all Disney employees are required to adhere to. These ethical standards include integrity, honestly, respect, quality service, personal responsibility, fairness, inclusiveness, and dignity. This strong ethical code of conduct has helped Disney develop a positive brand, create an amazing reputation, and experience tremendously sustainable and profitable success. In addition to the profitability success of Disney, this company was also voted number one by the Boston College Center for Corporate Citizenship 2009 Global Reputation Pulse Study, which is a testament to the power of ethical leadership.

In order to see the power of ethical leadership in your own leadership journey, you must first develop a set of ethical standards that you plan to act, live, and lead by. The ethical standards that you create may differ from others in certain situations, but the key for you as a leader is to promote ethical behavior by setting a good personal example of what you expect others to be accountable for within your organization or company. One of the main reasons this is important is that research has revealed that the best way to promote ethical behavior is by setting a good personal example because employees expect their leaders to enforce the proper standards and guidance for the organization. Now, once these ethical standards have become a part of who you are as a leader, you can expect to see some significant success as an ethical leader because research has shown that strong ethical leadership has a great impact on the financial health of different organizations and companies.

To help you begin this process of developing into an ethical leader, I have created a series of four questions for you to answer, develop, and discuss with your friends, mentors, and family members.

LEADERSHIP NOTES: _____

_____

_____

_____

_____

_____

_____

_____

_____

_____

_____

_____

_____

_____

_____

_____

_____

19

FOUR DISCUSSION QUESTIONS:
Are you an ethical leader?

QUESTION ONE

As a leader, what specific values must you develop within yourself in order to become an example of an ethical leader in your organization or company?

_____

_____

_____

QUESTION TWO

What specific things must you do in order to develop the specific values that are required of you as an ethical leader within your organization or company?

_____

_____

_____

QUESTION THREE

On a scale of 1–10, how effective are you at living out these ethical values as a leader within your organization or company? Please explain why you chose this answer.

_____

_____

_____

QUESTION FOUR

As the leader of your organization or company, what specific things can you do today in order to become more effective at serving as an ethical leader of your organization or company?

_____

_____

_____

LEADERSHIP QUESTION #20
Are you a resilient leader?

Throughout my leadership journey as a national speaker, author, and expert, I have always taken time to focus my efforts on discovering the common characteristics that separate good leaders from great leaders. Although many characteristics separate good leaders from great leaders, one of the most important leadership characteristics that I believe every leader must possess if they desire to become great and obtain personal, career, and leadership success is resilience. Resilience is a characteristic that Steve Jobs, Thomas Edison, Dr. Martin Luther King Jr., Winston Churchill, Nelson Mandela, Rosa Parks, Oprah Winfrey, and many other great leaders possessed—and it's a quality of leadership that enabled these leaders to do extraordinary things. Even though some people define resilience as an ability to cope with adversity and adapt to challenges or changing circumstances, I like to define resiliency as an ability to cope, adapt, endure, persevere, and overcome challenges, obstacles, failures, rejection, uncertainties, and fears that stand between you and your vision or dream.

Some of the primary reasons that it's vitally important for twenty-first century leaders to possess resiliency are that there will be new problems that will require new solutions, there will be challenges that will require leaders to endure and persevere, and there will be changes within our culture and society that will require leaders to change, adapt, and adjust. Resiliency is also crucial for twenty-first century leaders to possess because every leader will face disappointments, failure, rejection, uncertainty, and great challenges, and resilience is needed in order to overcome these inevitable challenging situations and circumstances.

Although it takes time to develop resilience, there are some specific things you can do in order to develop this leadership characteristic within yourself. The first step toward developing resilience as a leader is creating a proper perspective about challenges and adversity. In essence, instead of allowing the adversity or challenge to affect your state of being, you should focus on obtaining the lesson and opportunity that lies within every adverse and challenging situation. For example, when you fail, see it as preparation for success; when you get rejected, see it as direction toward something better; and when an obstacle seems very challenging, see it as an opportunity to grow and become a better leader and person.

Once you have the proper perspective about adverse and challenging situations, the next step you can take toward developing resiliency is becoming a leader who is a lifelong learner. In essence, instead of viewing every adverse or negative situation as the worst thing in the world, start looking for the lessons that can be discovered in these tough situations. The primary reason this aspect of the challenge is important is that the lessons you normally learn in adverse or challenging situations can be the things that help you reach your fullest potential as a leader. But, if you do not look for the lessons in the negative circumstances, you will miss the silver lining within the storm that was there to elevate you to the next level in your life.

And lastly, the final step you can take toward developing resiliency is learning how to encourage, motivate, and empower yourself when bad situations are occurring in your life. In essence, instead of focusing on the bad, as a leader, you must learn how to get to a place where you can encourage yourself, motivate yourself not to give up, and create a place of peace when chaos is surrounding you. Ultimately, when you are able to create this space in the tough moments, not only does it help you when things are going well, but it gives you the sustainable strength that you need to keep pushing forward when nothing seems to be going right in your life.

There are definitely more steps that can be taken to develop resiliency, but these are three specific steps that emerging leaders can take to develop greater resiliency as leaders. To help you begin this process of developing more resiliency as a leader, I have created a series of four questions for you to answer, develop, and discuss with your friends, mentors, and family members.

LEADERSHIP NOTES: _____

_____

_____

_____

_____

_____

_____

_____

_____

_____

_____

_____

_____

_____

_____

_____

20

FOUR DISCUSSION QUESTIONS:
Are you a resilient leader?

QUESTION ONE

On a scale of 1–10, how resilient are you as a leader of your organization or company? Please explain why you chose this answer.

_____

_____

_____

QUESTION TWO

Based on your response to the previous rating, what specific things must you do in order to become more resilient as a leader?

_____

_____

_____

QUESTION THREE

What specific things can you do on a daily basis to become more resilient as a leader?

_____

_____

_____

QUESTION FOUR

As the leader of your organization or company, what specific things can you do today in order to become more effective at displaying resiliency to the individuals who work with you?

_____

_____

_____

LEADERSHIP QUESTION #21
Are you an exceptional team player?

Some time ago, a friend and I were having an engaging discussion on the future of leadership among the Millennial Generation (those born between 1977–1994). During this candid conversation, my friend and I agreed that one of the keys to becoming an effective leader of the twenty-first century is being able to effectively work with others. In essence, leaders of the twenty-first century will not only need to be effective at working collectively with others, but they will need to understand how to effectively work within a team. Although every great leader in the past has been able to have a great impact in the world because of their ability to develop and work with an amazing team of people, in the twenty-first century, I believe that this leadership skill set will be more essential for leaders to possess than ever before.

I feel strongly about this particular stance on leadership because collective leadership is one of the leadership styles of the future, and research on the Millennial Generation has revealed that members of this generation are more interested in working together as a team than individually. In fact, not only do members of the Millennial Generation desire to work as a team, but according to research, they believe they can make more of a difference as a team. For example, in a Circle 2007 survey, Millennial participants were asked, "How much difference do you believe people working together as group can make in solving problems?" Shockingly, 92 percent of the people believed that working together as a group will make at least some difference, 62 percent stated that working together as a group would make a great deal of difference, and only 1 percent of people said that working together as a team would make no difference at all. When asked "How much difference do you believe you can personally make in solving problems?" 63 percent of people believed they could personally make at least some difference, but only 18 percent believed they could make a great deal of difference. In addition to this study, a 2007 Greenberg Millennial Study also revealed that approximately 63 percent of Millennials felt that the best way to address the challenges facing the country was "through a collective social movement." Essentially, what this means for emerging and seasoned leaders of the twenty-first century is that if you are going to be the world's next top leaders, you must become leaders who are exceptional team players.

I want to provide you with five specific things that I believe will help you transform into this exceptional team player as a leader. First, if you desire to develop into an exceptional team player, you must know your role within the group, and you must know how execute your role very well. Second, you must develop into a leader who authentically cares about the well-being of others and is willing to make personal sacrifices for the overall vision of the team. Third, you must be someone who is dependable and can be trusted to get the job done. Fourth, you must become effective at bringing different people together for a common purpose or cause. And lastly, you must respect everyone on the team, treat everyone on the team well, communicate and deal with conflict effectively, listen to the comments and concerns of everyone, and avoid pride and selfishness.

In essence, as the leader of a team, your job is to respect everyone, treat everyone well, communicate and deal with conflict effectively, listen to all the different concerns from each of the members, and make sure that you win and lose as a group versus individually. So many times, leaders fail to be exceptional team players because they allow their pride, selfishness, or ego to get in the way of the ultimate purpose of the team. Do not let this be you!

To help you begin this process of developing into an exceptional team player as a leader, I have created a series of four questions for you to answer, develop, and discuss with your friends, mentors, and family members.

LEADERSHIP NOTES: _____

_____

_____

_____

_____

_____

_____

_____

_____

_____

_____

_____

_____

_____

_____

_____

_____

_____

21

FOUR DISCUSSION QUESTIONS:
Are you an exceptional team player?

.

QUESTION ONE

On a scale of 1–10, how effective are you at working, leading, and serving as the member of a collective group of people? Please explain why you chose this answer.

_____

_____

_____

QUESTION TWO

Based on your response to the previous rating, what specific things must you do in order to become more effective at working, leading, and serving a collective group of people?

_____

_____

_____

QUESTION THREE

What specific things can you do on a daily basis to become more effective at working with, leading, and serving a collective group of people?

_____

_____

_____

QUESTION FOUR

As the leader of your organization or company, what specific things can you do today in order to see the positive results of a leader who is exceptional at working with a team of people?

_____

_____

_____

LEADERSHIP QUESTION #22
Are you leading with humility?

A few years ago, I had the opportunity to read an article in the Harvard Business Review that was written by Jim Collins, author of *From Good to Great,* about Level 5 Leadership. Level 5 Leadership is a concept that began in 1996 when Collins started researching what makes a company great and discovered that 11 of the 1,435 companies that were considered great became great because the leaders of these companies possessed Level 5 Leaders. Shockingly to me, one of the main characteristics of these great leaders was humility. In essence, according to Mr. Collins, the leaders who were able to have the greatest impact within all the companies he studied were those who led with humility and intense professional will. Although Mr. Collins discovered several other leadership qualities that leaders must possess in order to become Level 5 Leaders, these were the two main leadership qualities that separated the Level 5 Leader from the other four levels.

Following this eye-opening experience regarding leadership, I began to research and learn more about humility because I really wanted to develop a greater understanding of this concept as it relates to leadership. Thankfully, after a few hours of research on this leadership characteristic, not only did I discover what it meant to lead with humility, but I developed greater insight into why this leadership trait was so highly regarded by Mr. Collins. In my search to learn more about humility as it relates to leadership, I also found that individuals who are able to lead with humility must be secure in themselves, must have a heart for the betterment of people, must be totally invested in the vision of the company or organization, and must have an ability to do good for others regardless of the response to their positive actions.

One of the main reasons I believe that the four qualities listed above are critical for individuals to possess is that humble leaders are more focused on the tasks and people around them than they are on themselves. They credit others instead of themselves, have more ambition for the company's long-term success than their own, and don't seek success for their own glory. In addition, these leaders authentically have a heart to see people around them reach their fullest potential, blame themselves (not others) for a company's/organization's bad results, treat everyone with respect regardless of who the person is, and are confident without being prideful or cocky. These qualities are summed up in this powerful statement by author and management expert Ken Blanchard: "Humility does not mean you think less of yourself, it means you think of yourself less."

Throughout my life, I have met a variety of men and women who have been effective because of their humility. One of the greatest examples of humility has been a good friend of mine named DeVon Franklin. DeVon serves as one of the youngest African American vice presidents of production in Hollywood. He has also written a best-selling book entitled *Produced By Faith*, he has served as a keynote speaker at many different events all across the country, he has won multiple awards for his great work, he married an incredible actress, and he has been featured on many popular television and radio programs. Thankfully, with all this success at the age of 34, DeVon is still very down-to-earth, he treats everyone with the utmost respect regardless of who they are, and he makes it very clear in his presentations that success for him is not about the accolades—it's about making quality films that have a positive impact on the lives of others.

The attitude and lifestyle modeled by DeVon Franklin is a picture of what can happen in a leader's life when they make a concerted effort to lead with humility. To help you begin this process of developing into an individual who leads with humility, I have created a series of four questions for you to answer, develop, and discuss with your friends, mentors, and family members.

LEADERSHIP NOTES: _____

_____

_____

_____

_____

_____

_____

_____

_____

_____

_____

_____

_____

_____

_____

_____

_____

_____

22

FOUR DISCUSSION QUESTIONS:
Are you leading with humility?

QUESTION ONE

On a scale of 1–10, how effective are you at leading with humility?
Please explain why you chose this answer.

_____

_____

_____

QUESTION TWO

Based on your response to the previous rating, what specific things
must you do in order to become more effective at leading with
humility?

_____

_____

_____

QUESTION THREE

What specific things can you do on a daily basis to become more
effective at leading with humility?

_____

_____

_____

QUESTION FOUR

As the leader of your organization or company, what specific things
can you do today in order to see the positive results of leading with
humility?

_____

_____

_____

CHAPTER THREE
THE RELATIONAL LEADER

Some well-known leadership experts in higher education state that leadership has to do with relationships and is inherently a relational, communal process. Another leadership expert states that leadership is always dependent on the context and that the context is established by the relationship value. Personally, I agree with both views of leadership because I have found that great leaders of the past and present know how to effectively connect, build, empower, and inspire the groups of people whom they have been given the opportunity to serve as leaders. In order for emerging leaders to effectively do this in the twenty-first century, they must develop the specific skills needed to evolve into an amazing relational leader.

So, in this third chapter of the book, I have developed a set of eleven new questions that are specifically geared at helping you become an effective relational leader of the twenty-first century. This portion of the book will help you learn and reflect upon a series of questions that revolve around the characteristics of a relational leader in order to assist you in discovering some specific leadership skills that you must develop in order to effectively serve as a relational leader and evolve into one of the World's Next Top Leaders!

LEADERSHIP QUESTION #23
Are you an adaptable leader?

In the latter part of 2012, I was having a conversation with a good friend of mine from Sherwin-Williams who served as a Human Resource Manager in Denver, Colorado. During our in-depth discussion, I talked with him about the keys to career success in the twenty-first century, and I asked him about the professional skills that are most important for emerging leaders to develop while they are in college. Of all the different leadership skills that I thought my friend would mention in our conversation, he told me that adaptability was one of the most important skill sets that men and women must develop if they desire to obtain career leadership success in the twenty-first century. One of the main reasons he felt so strongly about this leadership skill set is that companies and organizations are not only constantly changing, but with the emergence of diversity, globalization, information, and the use of technology, leaders must be able to adapt quickly to the changes that will present themselves in different workplaces around the world. Just a few weeks after this conversation with my friend, I learned about a study done by Randstad (published in the *Huffington Post*) of 1,400 women in the workplace stating that flexibility and adaptability were the two skills needed most in the twenty-first century in order to obtain success in the workplace.

After learning about the importance of this skill set, I decided to do more research on adaptability as it relates to leadership. During my research, I learned that an adaptable leader is someone who knows how to mobilize people to tackle tough challenges, engage with anyone at any moment, navigate change and uncertain situations, and effectively follow their intuitive thoughts and feelings. In addition to the characteristics stated above, I discovered that an adaptable leader also understands how to deal with the different emotions of others, effectively be transparent with others, effectively lead and work with different types of people, and effectively adjust to changing situations and uncertain environments, and is a master at adjusting to different environments. In effect, an adaptable leader is someone who not only knows how to lead people through change and challenging circumstances, but who also knows how to easily adjust to different people, environments, and ways of doing things.

If emerging and seasoned leaders are going to further develop this skill set in the twenty-first century, there are a few things they can do to facilitate this process. The first thing that leaders can do to develop this skill set is increase their adaptive capacity, which scholars have defined as the ability to process new experiences to find their meaning and integrate those findings into one's life. In essence, developing your adaptive capacity means that you have an ability to effectively connect new experiences (including events, speakers, international business meetings, conversations, books, and vacations) to some aspect of your life as a leader so that those experiences become relevant to others around you. The second thing you must do to develop into an adaptable leader is to be tolerant of others, be open to different ways of thinking, be patient with others, and respect others' differences. Thirdly, you must be secure in who you are, and you must be a positive thinker because the confidence in who you are and the positive thinking will enable you to overcome the challenges that will manifest in your life when you attempt to become more adaptable. And the final thing you must do in order to develop into an adaptable leader is to learn how to be flexible in the face of change. In essence, adaptability is all about being flexible in the face of change, and if you are going to be flexible in the face of change, you must learn how to effectively change directions and ways of doing things at any moment.

To help you begin this process of developing into an adaptable leader, I have created a series of four questions for you to answer, develop, and discuss with your friends, mentors, and family members.

LEADERSHIP NOTES: _____
_____
_____
_____
_____
_____
_____
_____
_____
_____
_____
_____
_____
_____
_____
_____
_____
_____

23

FOUR DISCUSSION QUESTIONS:
Are you an adaptable leader?

QUESTION ONE

On a scale of 1–10, how effective are you at adapting to different environments, scenarios, and people as a leader? Please explain why you chose this answer.

_____

_____

_____

QUESTION TWO

Based on your response to the previous rating, what specific things must you do in order to become more effective at adapting to different environments, scenarios, and people as a leader?

_____

_____

_____

QUESTION THREE

What specific things can you do on a daily basis as a leader to become more adaptable as a leader within your organization or company?

_____

_____

_____

QUESTION FOUR

As the leader of your organization or company, if you choose to become more adaptable to different environments, scenarios, and people, what types of results do you plan to see happen in your life as a leader?

_____

_____

_____

LEADERSHIP QUESTION #24
Are you leading with love?

One of the most popular leadership concepts that I have been speaking about to various audiences all across the country over the past few years is the power of leading with love. This concept of leadership was first introduced to me several years ago when I had the opportunity to watch a leadership video on this concept created by leadership guru Kenneth Blanchard. In the video, Mr. Blanchard describes leading with love as treating people right, valuing the work of everyone connected to the business or organization, and leading with a heart of service. Furthermore, he explains that individuals who lead with love will succeed above their competitors, establish customer loyalty, experience greater levels of employee engagement, and position themselves for profitability year after year. After learning about this concept of leadership from Mr. Blanchard, I became interested in learning more about what it means to lead with love and how this concept of leadership could help me and others serve more effectively as leaders in the twenty-first century.

Thankfully, after a couple of years of research and practice, I was able to develop a greater understanding of this leadership concept. For instance, I was able to discover that leading with love was not just an emotional feeling, but it was an action that required emerging and seasoned leaders to forgive others, treat everyone with respect, be patient, show compassion, make sacrifices, respect and embrace the differences of others, and have a heart that desires the best for everyone regardless of who they are. I learned that the power of leading with love was exemplified most when an individual decided to make the choice to forgive, be patient with others, make sacrifices, and want the best for others regardless of how he or she felt on the inside about the particular situation or person. I found out that men and women who choose to lead with love despite their emotional feelings automatically alleviated some of the negativity that causes certain individuals to fail at becoming effective leaders of diverse groups of people. And lastly, I saw how the power of love enabled great leaders such as Dr. Martin Luther King Jr., Mother Teresa, and Jesus Christ to have a huge impact on the lives of people all across the world.

Like many of these great leaders from our past, if emerging and seasoned leaders make the choice to become more intentional about leading with love by applying different attributes of love to their leadership styles regardless of how they feel about people or a specific circumstance, not only will these men and women become more effective leaders in the twenty-first century, but they will also have an incredible impact on their community, nation, and world.

To help you begin this process of developing into an amazing leader who leads with love, I have created a series of four questions for you to answer, develop, and discuss with your friends, mentors, and family members.

24

FOUR DISCUSSION QUESTIONS:
Are you leading with love?

QUESTION ONE

What does it mean to lead with love?

_____

_____

_____

QUESTION TWO

On a scale of 1–10, how effective are you at leading with love? Please explain why you chose this answer.

_____

_____

_____

QUESTION THREE

Based on your response to the previous rating, what specific things must you do in order to become more effective at leading with love as a leader?

_____

_____

_____

QUESTION FOUR

What specific things can you do on a daily basis as a leader to become more effective at leading with love within your organization or company?

_____

_____

_____

LEADERSHIP QUESTION #25
Are you an effective networker?

Over the past ten years, I have been blessed with the opportunity to travel to many different college campuses all across the country as a national speaker, author, and leadership expert. One of the questions I get most often after my presentation is, "What do you believe are some of the greatest challenges facing leaders of the Millennial Generation (those born between 1977–1994)?" To answer this particular question, I briefly talk about the different social issues affecting our communities, nation, and world. I like to emphasize that our generation has to understand that emerging leaders will need to be courageous enough to do some things differently than past generations in order to succeed in the twenty-first century. And lastly, I like to tell various audiences that our generation of leaders will have to be more globally minded, more innovative, more courageous, more tech-savvy, and optimistic enough to pursue solutions to problems within our community, nation, and world that other generations have not been able to solve thus far.

In addition to the above answers, I also tell audiences that members of our generation must learn how to build positive relationship with others, develop powerful coalitions with different individuals and organizations, and effectively network with others. Some of the primary reasons I believe that it's vitally important for emerging leaders to learn how to effectively network with others are because emerging leaders who know how to network with different types of people will increase leadership effectiveness by deepening and broadening communication channels within organizations; they will remove political roadblocks that divide groups, people, and organizations; and they will uncover new opportunities for expansion and advancement. Leaders who know how to effectively network with others will also gain more exposure for the organization and themselves, they will strengthen their support and resource base, and unexpected positive opportunities will be made available to them because of their ability to network and build positive relationships with others.

Although there are many important facets of an effective networker, I want to share with you a set of key things that I believe every leader must possess in order to effectively network with others. First, leaders who desire to develop into effective networkers must love people. This quality is so important for leaders to possess because networking is all about conversing with others, getting to know different types of people, and being an authentic person who really cares about the people they are networking with. Second, leaders who desire to develop into effective networkers must develop a great reputation and a strong elevator pitch. These two qualities are important as they relate to networking because your reputation is key to establishing a credible and trustworthy relationship with people, and your elevator pitch is a quick thirty-second presentation that enables others to easily learn who you are. Thirdly, if you are going to be an effective networker, you must be strategic. The primary reason this quality is so important as it relates to networking is that effective networkers not only strategically build relationships with certain individuals and organizations, but they systematically create win-win relationships that benefit both parties involved. The fourth and fifth key things that every leader must possess in order to effectively network with others are courage and effective people skills. One of the main reasons that courage and effective people skills are important is that it takes courage to approach someone you have never met before, and it takes exceptional people skills to build positive relationships with people whom you desire to do business with in the future. Lastly, the final two things that are essential to effective networking are becoming someone who is authentic and who purposely adds value to the person you are choosing to network with. In essence, instead of just looking to obtain a favor from the person or organization you are networking with, it's critical that you think about ways that you can add more value to the person you are networking with than they can add to you. Ultimately, if you are able to do this with an authentic heart, you will be amazed at the results you will obtain as a networker.

Thankfully, these keys to networking have not only helped me serve as an effective leader, but they have also enabled me to see the positive results of networking. One of the stories that I often share with people occurred three years ago in Southern California. I was speaking at an event in Los Angeles and met a positive leader in my community. Although we never connected over the phone for three months following the event, we accidently ran into one another three months later at a local diner that was directly across the street from my house at the time. During this forty-five minute conversation, I learned about his personal ambitions and shared some my aspirations with him as well. By the end of the conversation, he connected me with a foundation in Long Beach that provided grant money for worthy causes. This unexpected connection enabled me to obtain a $10,000 grant that was used to provide one hundred student leaders with free scholarships to our first annual Circle of Change Leadership Conference. Because of this one connection, we have been able to host our annual Circle of Change Leadership Conference for four years now.

To help you begin this process of experiencing the benefits of networking, I have created a series of four questions for you to answer, develop, and discuss with your friends, mentors, and family members.

25

FOUR DISCUSSION QUESTIONS:
Are you an effective networker?

QUESTION ONE
What specific skills must you develop in your area of expertise in order to become an effective networker?

_____

_____

_____

QUESTION TWO
On a scale of 1–10, how effective do you believe you are at networking with others as a leader in your area of expertise? Please explain why you chose this answer.

_____

_____

_____

QUESTION THREE
Based on your response to the previous rating, what specific things must you do in order to become more effective at networking with others in your area of expertise?

_____

_____

_____

QUESTION FOUR
What specific things can you do on a daily basis as a leader to become more effective at networking with others within your area of expertise?

_____

_____

_____

LEADERSHIP QUESTION #26
Are you effective at managing relationships?

Approximately four years ago, we hosted our first annual Circle of Change Leadership Conference in Long Beach, California. During the conference, we had a special panel each evening that consisted of seasoned leaders and executives who shared their insights about effective leadership in their respective professions. Shockingly to me that night, the most popular skill set discussed by this esteemed group of leaders was the importance of being able to effectively manage relationships. All the leaders talked about other key leadership traits, but the most popular characteristic of leadership that many of these executives shared with the audience that night was relationship management.

According to these executives and leaders, effective management of relationships meant that leaders were not only effective at creating powerful partnerships and relationships with different individuals and organizations, but they were effective at managing the relationships as well. In essence, leaders who were effective at managing relationships were very good at meeting people, staying connected to the array of people they met, and providing value to those important relationships in their lives. As a result, they experienced great opportunities for advancement and promotion because of their effectiveness at managing these important relationships.

Although emerging and seasoned leaders can build, develop, and effectively manage relationships in many different ways, I want to provide you with four specific strategies that I believe will help you effectively manage key relationships in your life as a leader. First, if you desire to build, develop, and effectively manage a relationship, you must build it upon trust. Trust is a foundational pillar of every great relationship. It is established when others can depend upon you to get things done, when they view you as someone who lives with integrity (being a person of your word), when they perceive you as a responsible individual, and when your reputation with others is very positive. Secondly, you must be effective at establishing a common bond with others. In essence, as a leader, if you are going to effectively build, develop, and manage relationships with others, it's vitally important that you discover a common bond with others and build your relationships upon those common interests. For example, when I talk to various audiences about developing cross-cultural relationships, one of the first things I always tell them to do is to focus on the good rather than the negative and build upon the good things that you have in common with the other party. The primary reason I suggest this to various audiences is that I strongly believe that focusing on the good of others and sharing common interests is one of the simplest yet most powerful ways to develop common bonds and positive relationships with others.

Thirdly, if you are going to develop a strong relationship with others, you must have frequent communication. I do not mean that you have to contact someone every day, but I do believe it's important to stay in contact with the other person fairly often. The primary reason this is important as it relates to leadership is that frequent communication is one of the key tools that we use to create, build, and develop solid relationships. And the final skill set that you must possess in order to build, develop, and effectively manage your relationships with others is to constantly focus on ways that you can add value to others daily instead of just thinking about ways they can help you. In essence, instead of just seeking out ways that other people can help you advance, take the time to discover ways that you can help other people experience great success as well. The primary reason this is so important is because quality relationships are built, developed, and managed effectively with others when we become a valuable resource for helping others make their dream or vision a reality. This is why I believe Zig Ziglar once said, "You will get all you want in life if you help enough other people get what they want."

There are definitely more strategies that every leader can use to build, develop, and effectively manage relationships with others, but these are four specific strategies that I believe will help you become more effective in this aspect of your leadership development. To help you grow in this area, I have created a series of four questions for you to answer, develop, and discuss with your friends, mentors, and family members.

LEADERSHIP NOTES: _____

_____

_____

_____

_____

_____

_____

_____

_____

_____

_____

_____

_____

_____

_____

_____

_____

26

FOUR DISCUSSION QUESTIONS:
Are you effective at managing relationships?

QUESTION ONE

What specific skills must you develop in your area of expertise in order to become an effective manager of your key relationships?

_____

_____

_____

QUESTION TWO

On a scale of 1–10, how effective do you believe you are at building and managing relationships with others as a leader in your area of expertise? Please explain why you chose this answer.

_____

_____

_____

QUESTION THREE

Based on your response to the previous rating, what specific things must you do in order to become more effective at managing relationships with others in your area of expertise?

_____

_____

_____

QUESTION FOUR

What specific things can you do on a daily basis as a leader in order to become more effective at managing relationships with others in your area of expertise?

_____

_____

_____

LEADERSHIP QUESTION #27
Are you effective at resolving conflict?

Over the past decade, I have read and learned about hundreds of amazing leaders from various professional arenas. One of the common characteristics that I have noticed in these leaders is that they all had to overcome a challenge of some sort, depend on a group of people to help them manifest their vision or dream, and become effective at dealing with conflict. In essence, each of these great leaders of our past and present not only had to develop a great team of people around them and become very resilient in their leadership journey, but they had to learn how to effectively resolve conflicts. Some of the main reasons that these great leaders had to learn how to effectively resolve conflicts is because leaders who are unable to handle conflict experience personal dislikes among their team, negative working environments, constant bitterness and complaining, division among the team, and a terrible lack of synergy. On the other hand, leaders who have learned how to effectively resolve conflict within their organizations or groups served more effectively as leaders because they increased cohesion and synergy among the group, experienced more productive and positive work environments, increased understanding among the people in their group, and developed greater knowledge about themselves and others in the company or organization. Essentially, what this means for leaders of the twenty-first century is that if you are going to be effective at leading others within various organizations, workplaces, and groups, you must know how to effectively resolve conflict as a leader.

Although leaders are faced with different conflictual situations daily, one of the best ways to effectively resolve these situations as a leader in the twenty-first century is to become competent and knowledgeable about how to effectively respond and react to different conflicts that will arise in your company or organization. According to an online conflict management expert, there are five different ways that people can respond and react to conflict. The first way is by avoiding conflict altogether. In essence, instead of confronting the problem head-on, sometimes it's effective to avoid the conflict altogether by focusing on neutrality. Ultimately, the best time to use this strategy in a conflictual situation is when you feel the conflict is not a big deal, you feel the person is not going to ever give up on their stance, or you are not emotionally prepared to engage in an argument or discussion about a particular issue at a certain moment.

The second way that people deal with conflict, according to this conflict management expert, is through accommodation, which ultimately involves one of the individuals doing everything he or she can to make sure the other person is happy, regardless of the situation. This form of dealing with conflict is most effective when the conflict is minor or when tempers are extremely high.

The third way that people deal with conflict is through compromise. This form of conflict management involves both parties agreeing to be a little dissatisfied in order to reach a resolution. According to the conflict management expert, this is not an ideal way to deal with conflict over time because the dissatisfaction can become an issue again at some point, but it's a strategy that can be used for short-term disagreements and steps toward an ultimate resolution to the problem.

The fourth way that people deal with conflict is through competition and power. In essence, people who have a competitive mindset in conflict not only view the conflict as a game, but they attempt to win the battle by exerting their power in the situation. This style of dealing with conflict is most effective when this approach is necessary and when both parties understand the power they exert in the relationship. Personally, I am not fan of this strategy when it comes to leadership, but it is needed at certain moments in your leadership journey.

The fifth and final way that people deal with conflict, according to the conflict management expert, is through negotiation, which involves reaching a consensus about the conflict and working together to develop a solution to the problem. The expert considered this option to be the most effective way to deal with conflict because both parties develop a viable solution together, and they can both leave the conflictual situation satisfied with the outcome. I love this strategy the most because it's a win-win for both parties involved, and that is usually the goal of most people who engage in conflictual situations.

As leaders, if we learn how to effectively react and respond to conflictual situations, not only will we be more effective at managing different conflicts within our organizations, but we will be more effective at resolving conflicts as well. In addition to these different strategies of managing and resolving conflict as a leader, it's also important that you make sure that good relationships are the first priority, people and problems are kept separate, people are listening to one another, each interest is being stated in the situation, and decisions are made for the betterment of the group versus the individual. Ultimately, when this occurs, we will all become more effective at leading and resolving conflicts within our organizations, workplaces, and groups.

To help your grow in this area, I have created a series of four questions for you to answer, develop, and discuss with your friends, mentors, and family members.

27

FOUR DISCUSSION QUESTIONS:
Are you effective at resolving conflict?

QUESTION ONE

What specific skills must you develop in order to become more effective at resolving conflicts as a leader?

_____

_____

_____

QUESTION TWO

On a scale of 1–10, how effective do you believe you are at resolving conflicts as a leader in your area of expertise? Please explain why you chose this answer.

_____

_____

_____

QUESTION THREE

Based on your response to the previous rating, what specific things must you do in order to become more effective at resolving conflicts as a leader with others in your area of expertise?

_____

_____

_____

QUESTION FOUR

What specific things can you do on a daily basis as a leader in order to become more effective at resolving conflicts as a leader with others in your area of expertise?

_____

_____

_____

LEADERSHIP QUESTION #28
Do you have people competence?

Former President Theodore Roosevelt once said, "The single most important ingredient for success is knowing how to get along with people." John Rockefeller, one of the wealthiest men ever in American history, once said, "Good leadership consists of showing average people how to do superior work." Both of these quotes are important for men and women who desire to be one of the world's next top leaders to understand because among the foundational keys to becoming a great leader in the twenty-first century are being able to understand people, knowing how to get along with different types of people, and possessing an ability to get the most out of the people within your organization or company. One of the primary reasons this skill set is so important is because our organizations, companies, and workplaces are filled with people who possess different cultural backgrounds, personalities, religious beliefs, sexual orientations, gender differences, generational differences, and philosophies and perspectives on life. Furthermore, statistics have revealed that there are four different generations working together in the workplace for the first time ever; approximately one-third of the Millennial Generation come from a diverse background; 85% of the new workforce is women, minorities, or immigrants; 85% of conflict in the workplace is because of personality differences; and according to various studies on successful business practices, the most productive unit in business is a diverse unit. Essentially, what these facts point to is that if you're going to be an effective leader in the twenty-first century, not only is it vitally important that you are educated on how to lead and work with diverse groups of people, but it's also extremely important that you possess people competence. People competence is defined as being able to understand, work with, and get the most out of the diverse groups of people you have been given the responsibility to lead and serve with as a leader.

As leaders, if we are going to effectively execute this leadership skill, not only is it important that we are constantly educating ourselves about cultural, generational, gender, sexual, and personality differences within our area of influence, but it's also important that we are consistently taking the time to learn how to motivate these different types of people within our organizations, workplaces, and companies. One of the main reasons this strategy is important is because when we take time to develop this skill set, we become more knowledgeable about the differences that exist within our companies and organizations, and we learn how to diversify our leadership strategies in order to collectively inspire, motivate, and lead these different types of people within our sphere of influence as a leader. One scholar who focuses on generational diversity speaks to this point when he says, "Differences amongst the different generations require all leaders to have a style that is broad and flexible to each generation represented in the organization if they desire to succeed."

Although there are several different strategies that can be used to develop this leadership skill set, I like to focus on three specific things that every leader can do in order to become more effective at developing their people competence skills. The first thing that every leader can do to develop their people competence skills is to study different types of people by interacting with them, participating with them at different social events, stepping out of one's comfort zone, and making it a point to intentionally appreciate, embrace, and learn about the differences of others. The second thing that every leader must do, after they have made the decision to become a student of people, is to take the time to discover the secrets to inspiring, influencing, and persuading different types of people. In essence, instead of just learning about different types of people, as a leader of the twenty-first century, it's vitally important that you take the time to learn how to inspire, motivate, persuade, and influence these different types of people because this is an attribute of people competence and great leadership. Finally, once you have made a conscious effort to study people and learn about the secrets to motivating and inspiring them, you want to begin applying the lessons that you have learned in this developmental process because your growth in this specific area of leadership will only occur when you begin to use it as a leader. Moreover, as your people competence grows with the application of the things that you have learned about different types of people, your impact and effectiveness as a leader will grow and flourish as well.

To help you begin developing your people competence skills, I have created a series of four questions for you to answer, develop, and discuss with your friends, mentors, and family members.

LEADERSHIP NOTES: _____

_____

_____

_____

_____

_____

_____

_____

_____

_____

_____

_____

_____

_____

_____

_____

_____

_____

28

FOUR DISCUSSION QUESTIONS:
Do you have people competence?

QUESTION ONE

What specific things must you do in order to develop your people competence skills as a leader?

_____

_____

_____

QUESTION TWO

On a scale of 1¬–10, how well developed are your people competence skills? Please explain why you chose this answer.

_____

_____

_____

QUESTION THREE

Based on your response to the previous rating, what specific things must you do in order to become more effective with your people competence skills as a leader?

_____

_____

_____

QUESTION FOUR

What specific things can you do on a daily basis as a leader in order to become more effective at understanding different types of people and getting the most out of them within your company or organization?

_____

_____

_____

LEADERSHIP QUESTION #29
Are you a servant leader?

Approximately four years ago, I wrote a leadership book entitled *A Call to Action: 14 Highly Effective Leadership Principles for Leaders of Millennials*. In the book, I presented extensive research on the Millennial Generation (those born between 1977 – 1994), and I discussed fourteen research-based leadership traits that I believe leaders must possess if they desire to effectively influence, lead, and develop leaders of this emerging generation. One of the most important leadership models that I believe leaders must learn if they desire to effectively influence, lead, and develop leaders of this generation is the servant-leadership model that was created by Robert Greenleaf in 1977.

Although I like to define a servant-leader as someone who has an authentic heart to serve others, make others around them better, and make a positive impact in their community, nation, and world, Mr. Greenleaf defined this model of leadership as becoming a person who has an innate desire to lead by serving, serves out of alignment to his or her own beliefs, and strives to meet the highest priorities of others. Whether you choose to use Mr. Greenleaf's definition of the concept or mine, the reality is, if you are going to be an effective servant-leader, you must lead with a heart to serve others, you must be someone who has a heart to see the highest-priority needs of others on your team being met, you must base your success as a leader on the growth of others around you, you must exemplify moral excellence, and you must listen, empathize, empower the members of your team, and become someone who truly cares about the well-being of others. Essentially, if you can perfect these leadership attributes, you will experience the positive impact that transpires in an individual's life as a result of leading with the servant-leadership model.

Some of the main reasons I believe this leadership model is vitally important for leaders to possess in the twenty-first century are that servant-leaders add more value to the organization, they obtain more trust and credibility from others within the organization, they set a positive example for others to follow within the organization, and they will most likely make more of an impact on the people and the organization than others because they are committed to seeing the development of others around them. Moreover, this leadership model is key to effectively influencing, leading, and developing members of the Millennial Generation because research has revealed that a majority of members from this generation desire to be led by leaders who exemplify this leadership model. In addition to my personal beliefs about this leadership model, various studies have revealed that servant-leadership also positively affects subordinates' performance, it positively affects the organizational citizenship behavior, it positively affects the team effectiveness and confidence of the group, it causes people to go above and beyond their duties for the betterment of the organization, and it has a positive impact on the culture and society outside of the organization.

Companies such as The Toro Company, Herman Miller, Synovus Financial Corporation, The Men's Wearhouse, TDIndustries, and Southwest Airlines have been positively impacted by this leadership model. However, the greatest example of this leadership model for me is the life of Jesus Christ. The primary reason I believe he is the greatest example of this leadership model is because he not only talked about it during his life here on Earth, but his ability to lead with the servant-leadership model enabled him to create a worldwide movement with twelve people that has lasted 2,000-plus years. In essence, with twelve select people, this example of leadership has been able to create a movement that goes way beyond his years here on Earth. The powerful lesson we can all learn from this example is that the servant-leadership model helps the leader become more effective at leading people in the present and establishing a legacy that lasts well beyond their lifetime as a leader.

If you desire to develop into this type of leader in the twenty-first century, it's vitally important that you learn how to lead with the servant-leadership model. To help you grow in this area of leadership, I have created a series of four questions for you to answer, develop, and discuss with your friends, mentors, and family members.

LEADERSHIP NOTES: _____

_____
_____
_____
_____
_____
_____
_____
_____
_____
_____
_____
_____
_____
_____
_____
_____

29

FOUR DISCUSSION QUESTIONS:
Are you a servant leader?

QUESTION ONE

What specific things must you do in order to develop into an effective servant-leader?

_____

_____

_____

QUESTION TWO

On a scale of 1¬–10, how effective are you at applying the servant-leadership model to your personal leadership experience? Please explain why you chose this answer.

_____

_____

_____

QUESTION THREE

Based on your response to the previous rating, what specific things must you do in order to become more effective at leading with the servant-leadership model?

_____

_____

_____

QUESTION FOUR

What specific things can you do on a daily basis as a leader in order to become more effective at leading with the servant-leadership model within your company or organization?

_____

_____

_____

LEADERSHIP QUESTION #30
Are you a tech-savvy leader?

In today's work environment, this is the reality. Almost every individual who was born between 1977–1994 will spend one-third of their entire life on the Internet. By age 16, almost 74% of men and women born during this period of time will have access to a computer at home, and 94% of these individuals will be required to use the Internet for research projects at school. By 2020, IT jobs will increase by 22%, according to futurists, and certain experts within the entertainment industry are already making predictions that the celebrities of the future will be the online bloggers and social media rock stars who influence millions of followers online every day. In addition to these eye-opening statistics on technology, studies have revealed that 64% of the members of this emerging generation in America ask about social media policies during a job interview; almost 33% of individuals under 30 years of age in 2011 stated in a workplace study that they would be willing to take a pay cut for more social media freedom, device flexibility, and work mobility; and almost 43% of the members of this generation liked at least 20 brands on Facebook. Mix these tendencies with the workplace reality that by 2025, 75% of individuals of this generation will make up the workplace, and it becomes very clear that in order to be an effective leader of the twenty-first century, you must be tech-savvy.

There are many ways to describe a tech-savvy leader, but I like to describe a tech-savvy leader as someone who knows how to use, leverage, influence, and capitalize on the advancements of technology to accomplish their vision as a leader. In essence, an effective tech-savvy leader is someone who knows how to use and maximize the advancements of technology to lead others more effectively and efficiently. Although some people may argue that a leader does not need technology competence in order to serve as an effective leader, the reality is that with the emergence of technology in our society and culture, a leader does not have to be an expert in technology, but they must know how to incorporate it into their style of leadership. One of the main reasons this is vitally important as it relates to leadership is because efficient and sustainable companies and organizations of the twenty-first century not only have a great vision, strategic action plan, organizational structure, and effective leadership on different levels, but they also have a strong presence in the social media arenas. Moreover, leaders of these efficient, profitable, and sustainable organizations have also learned how to use technology as an effective way to communicate with members of their groups and teams.

There are many great examples of leaders who have been very successful at leading others because of their ability to utilize technology in their leadership style. One leader who stands out to me is a good friend who owns a successful marketing company in Southern California that specializes in innovation, branding, and web presence. This particular individual stands out to me because he has not only been able to use technology as a way to create a successful marketing business, book-publishing deal, multiple speaking engagements, and several successful annual events, but he has also been effective at leading others through technology. He communicates with his team online, holds various online discussions through chat rooms, stays connected to his followers through blogs and others social media outlets, and is effective at reaching others for various events that he hosts through online marketing campaigns. Moreover, he is an expert on technology and has continued to create multiple opportunities for himself as a leader because of his ability to incorporate technology into his leadership style.

Moving forward, these are the types of attributes that leaders of the future must possess if they are going to serve as effective leaders of the twenty-first century. So, to help your grow in this area as a leader, I have created a series of four questions for you to answer, develop, and discuss with your friends, mentors, and family members.

LEADERSHIP NOTES: _____

_____

_____

_____

_____

_____

_____

_____

_____

_____

_____

_____

_____

_____

_____

_____

_____

_____

30

FOUR DISCUSSION QUESTIONS:
Are you a tech-savvy leader?

QUESTION ONE

What specific things must you do in order to become more effective as a tech-savvy leader?

_____

_____

_____

QUESTION TWO

On a scale of 1–10, how effective are you at leading others through technology? Please explain why you chose this answer.

_____

_____

_____

QUESTION THREE

Based on your response to the previous rating, what specific things must you do in order to become more effective at leading others through technology?

_____

_____

_____

QUESTION FOUR

What specific things can you do on a daily basis as a leader in order to become more effective at leading others through technology within your company or organization?

_____

_____

_____

LEADERSHIP QUESTION #31
Are you an inspirational leader?

Vince Lombardi, former championship coach of the Green Bay Packers, once said, "Leadership is based on a spiritual quality; the power to inspire, the power to inspire others to follow." I agree with Vince Lombardi because when you think about leaders such as Dr. Martin Luther King Jr., Mother Teresa, Winston Churchill, Steve Jobs, Cesar Chavez, President Barack Obama, John F. Kennedy, Nelson Mandela, Oprah Winfrey, Margaret Thatcher, and many other influential leaders of our past and present, you will find that they all had an ability to inspire others to action. It seems as though almost every great leader of our past and present became known and celebrated because of their strong ability to inspire, motivate, and empower others to act, believe, and perform at higher levels for a specific vision, dream, or cause. Similar to these leaders of our past and present, if we are going to emerge and develop into the world's next top leaders, we must know how to effectively inspire, motivate, and empower others to act, believe, and perform at higher levels of excellence for a specific vision, dream, or cause.

One of the primary reasons that inspirational leaders will always be required within every generation is because when crisis, challenge, or adversity manifests in the lives of a generation or group of people, the inspirational leaders are the ones who enable people to rise up and overcome some of the greatest challenges that life can bring upon a generation or group of people. The second reason that inspirational leaders are needed is because people not only desire to be motivated and empowered, but there are certain levels of success that individuals will not be able to reach unless they have some form of inspiration in their lives. And finally, the last reason I believe inspirational leaders are required within every generation or group of people is because inspired leaders keep others engaged, help others see the purpose of their actions, and are able to bring out the best in others around them as well, which leads toward effective leadership within any area of expertise.

Although there are many different strategies that people use to help others develop into inspirational leaders, I want to provide you with seven specific strategies that I have found to help me effectively inspire others as a motivational speaker and leader. The first strategy that I believe every individual must use as a leader if they desire to inspire others is to be just as passionate about the vision as you are requiring others to be. In essence, as the leader, you want to have as much or more passion about the vision as you desire the other members of your organization or company to possess. The main reason this is important is because people are more inclined to be passionate about something when they see the person "selling" them the vision or dream exemplifying that same passion. The second and third strategies that leaders who desire to inspire others must use are to create an inspired shared vision and establish a set of powerful reasons why others must be as passionate about the vision or dream. These things are important for leaders to do because an inspired shared vision and an established set of passionate reasons why people should support a cause provide people with a stronger connection to your cause or desired outcome, and they're among the key elements that every great leader of our past and present has used to inspire, motivate, and empower others.

The fourth strategy that every leader must use in order to inspire others is to take time to learn about the people they are leading and discover specifically what things they can do or say in order to effectively connect with each person. In sports, you hear coaches talk about this all the time because one of their responsibilities is to motivate and inspire their team. But, in order to effectively do this, every great coach knows that they must learn what buttons to push within their players in order to get the most out of them. This same concept applies when it comes to leading others outside of the sports arena. The fifth and sixth strategies that every leader must do in order to inspire others are to constantly encourage the members of their team and think of ways to effectively challenge team members to reach new heights. In essence, every leader who desires to effectively inspire others must encourage, appreciate, and think of innovative and effective ways to challenge the members of their team daily. Lastly, the final strategy that every leader must use if they desire to become an inspirational leader is to become an example to others. In effect, as the leader, not only do you want to inspire and motivate others through your words, but your actions should back up your words as well because your actions are the key to connecting, inspiring, and motivating others. This is why I believe President Bill Clinton said, "As we have throughout this century, we will lead with the power of our example, but be prepared, when necessary, to make an example of our power." He understood the power that comes to a leader when he or she makes the effort to lead by example.

To help you grow into an inspirational leader, I have created a series of four questions for you to answer, develop, and discuss with your friends, mentors, and family members.

LEADERSHIP NOTES: _____

_____

_____

_____

_____

_____

_____

_____

31

FOUR DISCUSSION QUESTIONS:
Are you an inspirational leader?

QUESTION ONE
What specific things must you do in order to become more effective as an inspirational leader?

_____

_____

_____

QUESTION TWO
On a scale of 1–10, how effective are you at inspiring others? Please explain why you chose this answer.

_____

_____

_____

QUESTION THREE
Based on your response to the previous rating, what specific things must you do in order to become more effective at inspiring others?

_____

_____

_____

QUESTION FOUR
What specific things can you do on a daily basis as a leader in order to become more effective at inspiring others within your company or organization?

_____

_____

_____

LEADERSHIP QUESTION #32
Are you a socially competent leader?

In 2011, Daniel Goldman, coauthor of *Primal Leadership: Leading with Emotional Intelligence,* wrote an article on social competence in the Harvard Business Review Blog Network. In the article, Mr. Goldman talked about a CEO who was hired by a well-known company because the individual was a first-rate economist, had a spectacular resume, and did extremely well on all the interviews. Unfortunately for this CEO, within seven months, he was fired from the position because he had zero social intelligence, lacked interpersonal skills, and was unable to effectively manage relationships. In essence, although the CEO was extremely qualified for the position, his lack of social competence caused him to fail as a leader in this high-level position. Sadly, this sort of failure was not just a problem for this particular CEO—it's a problem that many leaders will have to face if they are not socially competent. Essentially, what this story teaches us is that if we are going to reach our fullest potential as leaders in the twenty-first century, not only must we have strong competence in our area of expertise, but we must have amazing social competence as well.

Although there are many definitions of a socially competent person, I like to define a socially competent leader as someone who has an ability to communicate, negotiate, decrease conflict, develop strong bonds, and achieve personal goals in various social interactions while also maintaining positive relationships with others. In essence, a social competent leader is someone who is able to build quality relationships with others, attain social goals in specific social contexts, achieve desired outcomes and adaptability in different social settings, perform well socially in different social and cultural settings, and maintain positive relationships with others in various social settings. Moreover, this type of leader not only has an amazing ability to connect and develop meaningful and positive relationships with various people regardless of their unique background, but they know how to effectively respond to the different behaviors, emotions, and interpersonal communication of others in different social settings. Basically, this type of leader knows how to access people and different social settings quickly while also adapting their style of interpersonal communication to effectively connect and develop positive relationships with others.

Ultimately, if we are going to develop this leadership skill set, there are five key things we must consider and develop within ourselves. The first thing we must do if we're going to become more socially competent as leaders is to learn how to regulate and manage our emotions and the emotions of others. In essence, as leaders, we must know how to control our emotions in various circumstances and learn how to respond effectively to other people's emotional expression in different social settings. The second thing we must do in order to develop our social competence is to become effective at understanding different social settings and knowing how to properly interact with others in various social gatherings. For example, your social responses to your family members at a family reunion will be different from your responses to potential clients at an important business dinner. Thirdly, if you are going to develop into a socially competent leader, you must develop awareness and knowledge of different social settings, environments, and behaviors that are expected in various social circles. And finally, as a socially competent leader, not only is important for you to develop strong interpersonal and social skills, but it's also important that you become aware of the different behaviors, cultural norms, and languages that can have an effect on your social interactions with others in various situations and circumstances.

An amazing example of this concept takes place in the biblical story of Daniel. Daniel was a Hebrew boy who was chosen to serve in the king's palace with three other Hebrew boys because he was good looking, gifted in wisdom and knowledge, quick to understand, and able to serve in the king's palace and teach the language of the king, which was different from his own language. Although there are numerous lessons related to career leadership success in this story, the most powerful aspect of this story to me as it relates to the social competent leader is the fact that Daniel and the other Hebrew boys were selected to serve in the king's palace because of their abilities. Although they were raised in a different environment, they had enough social competence to adapt, connect, evolve, and build positive relationships with other in their new social environment and setting. Essentially, what this means for emerging leaders of the twenty-first century is that in order to succeed, we must possess the social competence to adapt, connect, and effectively build positive social relationships in unique social settings.

To help you develop your social competence as a leader, I have created a series of four questions for you to answer, develop, and discuss with your friends, mentors, and family members.

LEADERSHIP NOTES: _____

_____

_____

_____

_____

_____

_____

_____

_____

_____

_____

_____

_____

_____

32

FOUR DISCUSSION QUESTIONS:
Are you a socially competent leader?

QUESTION ONE

What specific things must you do in order to become more effective as a socially competent leader?

_____

_____

_____

QUESTION TWO

On a scale of 1–10, how socially competent are you as a leader? Please explain why you chose this answer.

_____

_____

_____

QUESTION THREE

Based on your response to the previous rating, what specific things must you do in order to become more socially competent as a leader?

_____

_____

_____

QUESTION FOUR

What specific things can you do on a daily basis as a leader in order to become more socially competent within your company or organization?

_____

_____

_____

LEADERSHIP QUESTION #33
Are you a globally competent leader?

A few years ago, I was having a discussion with one of my friends about generational diversity and leadership. During this engaging and insightful discussion, my friend began to communicate with me about Generation Z, the generation that would follow the Millennial Generation and begin to emerge in America over the next ten to fifteen years. He stated that this emerging generation will lack interpersonal skills, be highly competent in all forms of technology and social media platforms, and possess several similar characteristics of the Millennial Generation. They will also be more globally aware than previous generations because of the advancements in technology. In essence, although many members of the previous three generations have grown in global awareness over the past thirty-plus years, my friend made the prediction that members of Generation Z will be more globally aware at their age than any previous generation because of the development of our society in the twenty-first century. Personally, I thought this was a great thing for this emerging generation because in order to succeed as a leader in the twenty-first century, it's vitally important that you evolve and develop into a globally competent leader.

According to the Florida International University Global Leadership Program, a globally competent leader is someone who accepts responsibility and active world citizenship; recognizes that people's well-being is interconnected and globally interdependent; exhibits awareness of his or her own cultural values, beliefs, attitudes, biases, and stereotypes, and the impact of these on others; acknowledges and has respect for the existence of different cultural values, beliefs, and attitudes; practices collective leadership methods that focus on inclusion, collaboration, and crossing boundaries; and seeks knowledge about world history, current events, global economics, and sustainability. Some of the mains reasons that many leadership experts agree that globally competent leaders are needed more than ever in the twenty-first century are because the world is becoming more globally connected than ever before, organizations and companies are becoming more culturally diverse than in years past, and leaders who desire to be effective in the twenty-first century must know how to interact, connect, and lead people from different cultural backgrounds. I believe this is why Jack Welch, former CEO of General Electric, once said, "The Jack Welch of the future cannot be me. I spent my entire career in the United States. The next head of General Electric will be somebody who spent time in Bombay, in Hong Kong, in Buenos Aires. We have to send our best and brightest overseas and make sure they have the training that will allow them to be the global leaders who will make GE flourish in the future."

Thankfully, experts such as *Chin, Gu, and Tubbs* have developed a Global Leadership Competency Model that helps people grow, evolve, and develop cultural intelligence, which is key to becoming a globally competent leader. This model has six specific levels. On the first level, leaders become aware of the cultural differences and norms in the world. Once this knowledge is attained, they move on to the second level, where they begin to develop a greater understanding of cultural differences by reading, observing, asking questions, and experiencing real life with these different world cultures. Following this level comes the third level, where individuals begin to show appreciation for the differences of other cultures by developing tolerance for these cultural differences and embracing the good that every culture around the world has to offer others.

By the time leaders evolve through the first three levels, they begin to accept these cultural norms and differences at the fourth level by recognizing commonalities, dealing with differences effectively, and increasing their appreciation for cultural differences among others. On the fifth level of this growth process, they internalize these positive behaviors of cultural competence and gain a clear sense of self-understanding, which leads to readiness to act and interact with the locals/nationals in a natural, appropriate, and culturally effective manner. And finally, the sixth and final levels of this model are the adaption stage. At these levels, not only has cultural competence become a way of life, but emerging leaders know how to gather knowledge and information about different cultures, and they know how to effectively adapt their behavioral patterns positively and effectively to the different cultural norms and differences in the world. Ultimately, once these skills are fully developed, leaders not only become more effective at working and leading people from different cultural backgrounds, but they also evolve into more responsible and effective global citizens.

To help you develop into a globally competent leader, I have created a series of four questions for you to answer, develop, and discuss with your friends, mentors, and family members.

LEADERSHIP NOTES: _____

33

FOUR DISCUSSION QUESTIONS:
Are you a globally competent leader?

QUESTION ONE
What specific things must you do in order to become more effective as a globally competent leader?

_____

_____

_____

QUESTION TWO
On a scale of 1–10, how globally competent are you as a leader? Please explain why you chose this answer.

_____

_____

_____

QUESTION THREE
Based on your response to the previous rating, what specific things must you do in order to become more globally competent as a leader?

_____

_____

_____

QUESTION FOUR
What specific things can you do on a daily basis as a leader in order to become more globally competent within your company or organization?

_____

_____

_____

CHAPTER FOUR
THE SPIRITUAL LEADER

When you think about leaders such as Dr. Martin Luther King Jr., Mahatmi Gandhi, Mother Teresa, George Washington, and other famous leaders who have had a significant positive impact on our communities, nation, and world, you will find that each of these leaders possessed a strong spiritual foundation. One expert on spirituality and social change describes the spiritual qualities that make up a strong spiritual foundation as higher consciousness, transcendence, self-reliance, love, faith, enlightenment, community, self-actualization, compassion, and forgiveness. This spiritual foundation affects the thoughts and behaviors of leaders in such a positive way that it broadens their self-concept, increases the role of morality, and strengthens the individual sense of responsibility toward the world. Essentially, what these experts and examples of effective leadership can teach us is that whether or not they believed in God, many men and women throughout history have had an enormous impact on the world because they developed a strong spiritual foundation as a leader.

So, in this fourth chapter of the book, I have developed a set of seven questions that are specifically geared at helping you develop a strong spiritual foundation for leadership success in the twenty-first century. The questions that are posed in this portion of the book will not only help you learn and reflect upon a series of questions that revolve around the characteristics of a spiritual leader, but they will also assist you in discovering some specific leadership skills that you must develop in order to create a strong spiritual foundation and evolve into one of the World's Next Top Leaders!

LEADERSHIP QUESTION #34
Do you know your purpose in life?

Approximately ten years ago, Pastor Rick Warren released a best-selling book entitled *The Purpose Driven Life.* This daily devotional book has not only impacted the lives of millions of people all across the world, but it has also become the second-highest-selling nonfiction book in publishing history, right behind the Bible. One of the main reasons I believe this book has done so well is because at some point in life, every individual will ask themselves the question, "What is my purpose in life, or why was I created to live here on Earth?" For some, this question will be easy to answer, while others will have a difficult time answering this question because discovering your purpose in life can be one of the most challenging things to uncover in your personal life. However, the more I have researched and studied some of the greatest leaders of all time, the more I have discovered that each of them was able to have an enormous impact on the world because they were clear about their calling and purpose in life. In essence, almost every great leader I have ever studied over the past fifteen years has been fairly clear about their life assignment as a leader. Similar to these amazing leaders of the past and present, if you're going to serve as one of the world's next top leaders, it is vitally important that you are aware of the fact that you were born with a purpose, and it's even more important that you discover that purpose for your life as a leader.

It's important for you to discover your purpose in life because your purpose will provide you with the passion, drive, meaning, strength, and excitement that have enabled great leaders to accomplish amazing things in the world. This is why I believe Steve Jobs, the founder of Apple, said, "For the past 33 years, I have looked in the mirror every morning and asked myself: 'If today were the last day of my life, would I want to do what I am about to do today?' And whenever the answer has been 'No' for too many days in a row, I know I needed to change something." Mr. Jobs knew about the power that comes to a leader who understands his or her purpose in life.

The second reason I personally believe it's very important for leaders to discover their purpose in life is because leaders who are living their purpose will not only have more of an impact as a leader, but they will also have a better attitude and will enjoy life more than individuals who do not have an idea of their purpose in life. This is probably why Helen Keller said, "Many people have the wrong idea of what constitutes true happiness in life because it is not attained through self-gratification, but it's obtained through fidelity to a worthy purpose." She understood that the true essence and happiness of life are obtained when you are able to discover your purpose in life. Essentially, if these two amazing leaders are correct in their assessment of life, it should be quite clear to us that we should all take the time to reflect, investigate, and take the necessary steps toward discovering our purpose in life as a leader.

For the past fifteen years, one of my missions as a national speaker and author has been to help others discover their purpose. Throughout this process, I have discovered that the sole purpose of every human being is to make the lives of others around them better by becoming who they were destined to be on Earth. Furthermore, the path to discovering one's purpose is different for everyone and transpires at different moments in people's lives. However, in this journey toward helping people discover their purpose in life, I have found that certain questions can help people move closer to finding their purpose in life. You have already answered the first three questions that I like to ask people in the first chapter of the book, which are: *What are your talents and strengths? What are you passionate about? What are your values?* The other four questions that I believe are important for each individual to ask themselves as they relate to purpose are: *In what ways do you like to serve and help others? What professional career would you do for free? Do you have a relationship with God? How can you use all these six questions that we have discussed in this portion of the book to have an impact on the world as a leader?* In essence, once you discover your strengths and talents, your passion, your values, how you like to help others, and what professional career you would do for free as well as create a relationship with God, the next step is to figure out how you can have an impact on the world by using the answers to the previous six questions.

Although there are other paths that people can use to find their purpose in life, the reason that I feel these final four questions are just as important as the first three questions as they relate to your purpose in life is because I believe that our purpose in life is placed in us at birth by God, and the core aspect of that purpose is to help others and make the world a better place. In addition, I believe that our purpose in life is so much a part of who we are that we would be inclined to pursue our purpose at all costs whether or not we made money at it. Therefore, if we are going to discover this purpose, not only is it important to have a relationship with the creator of that purpose and discover a professional career that we would do for free, but it's even more important to understand that the reason we have purpose is because we are meant to help or serve others and make the world a better place. Essentially, once you answer these seven questions, you will begin moving closer toward discovering your purpose in life as a leader and seeing the amazing manifestations that will occur for you when you are living out your purpose here on Earth.

To help you discover your purpose in life, I have created a series of four questions for you to answer, develop, and discuss with your friends, mentors, and family members.

34

FOUR DISCUSSION QUESTIONS:
Do you know your purpose in life?

QUESTION ONE

What are your top three strengths, talents, passion, and values in life as a leader? You should be able to easily answer this question.

_____

_____

_____

QUESTION TWO

What are three professional careers that you would do for free?

_____

_____

_____

QUESTION THREE

What are the three most exciting ways that you like to help and serve others as a leader?

_____

_____

_____

QUESTION FOUR

How can you use your strengths, talents, passion, values, strong desire to help others, and professional career that you would do for free in order to have an impact on the world as a leader?

_____

_____

_____

LEADERSHIP QUESTION #35
Are you pursuing something bigger than yourself?

Approximately three years ago, I was giving a keynote presentation in Miami, Florida. Following my keynote presentation at Broward College earlier in the afternoon, I decided to visit a friend of mine named Rich Wilkerson Jr., who serves as a youth pastor of Trinity Church in Miami. At the end of a powerful sermon he delivered on legacy, Rich took some additional time at the end of the service to show a ten-minute speech that was given by Dr. Randy Pausch on the *Oprah Winfrey Show*. During this impactful and inspiring presentation, Dr. Pausch not only talked about the importance of taking advantage of every day you have to live here on Earth, but he also talked about the power of legacy. In essence, as a man who was just days or weeks away from losing his life to a deadly disease, he shared with a huge television audience that we should appreciate life every day and we should do our part in making the world a better place. His personal contribution was giving this powerful lecture and sharing some words of wisdom with his children before he passed away so that they could have something to remember him by when they got older.

For me personally, this was a powerful moment that I will never forget because it was not only a moving and extremely inspirational message, but it also reaffirmed to me the importance of being a leader who is concerned about more than just personal success—who is concerned about creating something bigger than myself that can benefit future generations. My entire attitude as a leader changed because I realized that being a great leader was about using the present circumstances to create things that have long-lasting impact beyond my experience as the leader of an organization, company, or group of people. After discovering the power of pursuing something much bigger than myself as a leader, I began to discover that some of the greatest leaders of all time became amazing leaders because they were able to create a legacy that was bigger than themselves.

For example, when I think about the life of Dr. Martin Luther King Jr., one of the main reasons I believe he was considered such an amazing leader is because he was able to effectively lead a movement that millions of Americans are benefiting from today because he pursued a vision so much bigger than himself. Another great example of this concept is Mother Teresa, who not only gave her life for the betterment of the poor and disenfranchised, but in her day, she was willing to pursue a vision that was much bigger than her and would impact the lives of future generations. Like these great spiritual leaders of our past, if we are going to develop into amazing leaders of the twenty-first century and have a significant impact on our community, nation, and world, it's vitally important that we have a desire to create a positive legacy and pursue visions and dreams that are bigger than ourselves.

In order to effectively pursue a vision that is bigger than ourselves as leaders, not only is it important that we are not selfish leaders, but it's also vitally important that we authentically create and pursue a huge shared vision that is focused on making the world a better place and impacting the lives of future generations. In essence, leaders who are authentically pursing a vision that is bigger than themselves are more concerned about the sustainability of the vision and the people involved with the vision than their individual self. Ultimately, when leaders effectively create this type of vision and purpose for themselves, they reach higher levels of success, impact the lives of more people than they could have ever imagined, and most importantly, leave their mark as a leader.

To help you create a vision bigger than yourself, I have created a series of four questions for you to answer, develop, and discuss with your friends, mentors, and family members.

LEADERSHIP NOTES: _____

_____

_____

_____

_____

_____

_____

_____

_____

_____

_____

_____

_____

_____

_____

_____

_____

35

FOUR DISCUSSION QUESTIONS:
Are you pursuing something bigger than yourself?

QUESTION ONE

What would you consider to be a vision that is bigger than you?

_____

_____

_____

QUESTION TWO

As a leader of people, would you consider your current vision bigger than you? In essence, is your vision so big that it will impact the lives of others beyond your time as a leader of these people or this group, organization, or company?

_____

_____

_____

QUESTION THREE

If your vision is not bigger than you, what modifications can you make to your vision in order to create something that is bigger than you?

_____

_____

_____

QUESTION FOUR

What specific legacy do you plan to leave with your people, group, organization, or company after you have completed your service as a leader?

_____

_____

_____

LEADERSHIP QUESTION #36
Do you have an active prayer life?

When I was younger, my grandmother used to make three powerful statements that I have never forgotten for my entire life. These three statements were, "A family that prays together, stays together," "God may not answer your prayers when you desire them to be answered, but he is always on time," and "Prayer changes things." Although I didn't really think deeply about these powerful statements made by my grandmother when I was a child, as I grew older I began to discover that my grandmother was not only correct, but also that these words of wisdom were among the greatest advice I ever received in my entire life. The primary reason I feel so strongly about these three wise statements from my grandmother is because my prayer life has been the foundational piece of my success as a person, professional, and leader, and my prayer time has led me to amazing ideas and insights, miraculous interventions that shock me every time I think about them, and strength to overcome my greatest challenges in life.

Even though some people do not believe in prayer, I have discovered through my research that some of the greatest leaders of all time were able to do amazing things because they had a prayer life. For example, Mahatma Gandhi, Dr. Martin Luther King Jr., Mother Teresa, the Pope, Desmond Tutu, and many other great leaders who have had a huge impact on the world were all able to do so because they were men and women of prayer. In addition to these amazing leaders who obtained great success because of their prayer life, I have also heard countless stories about other leaders with various areas of expertise talk about how prayer opened up career opportunities of a lifetime, provided guidance in some of the most difficult situations, led toward greater success in their professional careers, helped them overcome great challenges as a leader, and positively impacted the lives of others around them as well.

For years, there has been a lot of discussion on the topic of prayer. Personally, I believe that many of the definitions used to describe prayer are great, but in my life, I have discovered that prayer is not only a time when you ask God to intervene in a specific situation within your life, but it's also a time of thanksgiving unto God, it's a time of declaring God's word over your life, it's a time of reflection about various things in your life, it's a time when you have a conversation with God about different things, it's a time when you ask for God's forgiveness in certain areas of your life, and it's a time to sit back and hear what God has to share with you. In essence, although the foundational aspect of prayer can best be described as communion with God, the impact of prayer manifests most when we take the time to create an active lifestyle of prayer that involves connecting with God on a daily basis.

Even though my prayer time was not long at all during the early years of life, as I have matured in this area and discovered the power of prayer, I have learned how to actively use the model of prayer that Jesus laid out for his disciples in the Bible and have seen tremendous results from this model of prayer in every aspect of my life. As future leaders of the twenty-first century, I am not expecting others to pray as much as I do on a daily basis, but I do believe that men and women who take the time to create an active lifestyle of prayer will see greater results in their personal, leadership, and career success.

To help you grow in this spiritual aspect of leadership, I have created a series of four questions for you to answer, develop, and discuss with your friends, mentors, and family members.

> "The great people of the earth today are the people who pray, (not) those who talk about prayer.but I mean those who take time and pray."
>
> ~ S.D.Gordon

LEADERSHIP NOTES: _____

_____

_____

_____

_____

_____

_____

_____

_____

_____

_____

_____

_____

_____

_____

_____

_____

_____

36

FOUR DISCUSSION QUESTIONS:
Do you have an active prayer life?

QUESTION ONE

What specific things must you do in order to create a more effective prayer life?

_____

_____

_____

QUESTION TWO

On a scale of 1–10, how effective is your prayer life? Please explain why you chose this answer.

_____

_____

_____

QUESTION THREE

Based on your response to the previous rating, what specific things must you do in order to create a more effective prayer life?

_____

_____

_____

QUESTION FOUR

What specific things can you do on a daily basis as a leader in order to see the positive results of an active prayer life?

_____

_____

_____

LEADERSHIP QUESTION #37
Do you believe in social justice?

People often ask me the question, "Who do you believe is the greatest leader of all time?" I immediately tell them that I believe Jesus was the greatest leader of all time. I believe Jesus was the greatest leader of all time because he created a legacy/movement that has spanned the world for 2,000-plus years with only 12 men, he gave his life for the well-being of the people who wrongfully accused him, he impacted the lives of many people beyond his years here on earth, and most importantly, he was a man who authentically cared about the disadvantaged, poor, sick, overlooked individuals and the social injustices that affect the lives of people around the world. In essence, Jesus was not only a leader who was concerned about fulfilling his own personal mission and purpose here on Earth—he was someone who deeply cared about justice for all of humanity. Like Jesus, if we are going to develop into amazing spiritual leaders, we must stand up for the less fortunate, and we must also be concerned about the social injustices that affect the lives of people within our communities, nation, and world.

For the past decade, I have heard about many amazing people who do incredible work in the area of social justice. Although this type of work has many different definitions and meanings behind it as it relates to leadership, I like to describe a leader who believes in social justice as someone who is concerned about fairness, doing the right thing, equality for all people regardless of their diverse background, loving one another, complete respect for all of humanity, and a compassionate heart to make sure that everyone is treated right in all matters. In essence, this type of leader cares about poor people, ending human trafficking in various parts of the world, stopping the bullying that occurs on campuses throughout America, stopping the oppression and prejudices in various aspects of our society, how we treat our environment, and people everywhere who are treated unjustly. In addition, this type of leader has a strong desire to make sure that everyone has access to the amazing opportunities that are available to us in our culture and society.

Unfortunately, at times, this type of leadership can be tough to live out because it requires sacrifices, it requires complete service to others, it requires you to give of yourself with no expectation of any return for your work, and it can make things uncomfortable in your life and lead to some incredible challenges because of the resistance that may occur in various situations. However, the wonderful thing about this type of leadership is that most of the leaders who have had an enormous impact on our world were able to do so because they were willing to fight against injustices that were experienced by certain groups of people. For example, Dr. King fought for the rights of people of color, Susan B. Anthony fought for the rights of women, Cesar Chavez fought for the rights of farm workers, Mother Teresa fought for the rights of the poor, and Florence Kelly fought for the rights of children. In addition, many other incredible leaders have had a huge impact on the world because they fought for justice within our communities, nation, and world.

Moving forward into the twenty-first century, there are going to be more injustices within our culture and society. As men and women who aspire to become the world's next top leaders, it's critical that we believe in and support issues that revolve around social justice because that is one of the foundational qualities and responsibilities of spiritual leaders who truly desire to have an impact on their community, nation, and world.

To help you grow in this spiritual aspect of leadership, I have created a series of four questions for you to answer, develop, and discuss with your friends, mentors, and family members.

> *"In days of difficulty, Americans everywhere must and shall choose the path of social justice., the path of faith, the path of hope, and the path of love toward our fellow man."*
>
> **~ Franklin D. Roosevelt**

LEADERSHIP NOTES: _____

_____

_____

_____

_____

_____

_____

_____

_____

_____

_____

_____

_____

_____

_____

_____

37

FOUR DISCUSSION QUESTIONS:
Do you believe in social justice?

QUESTION ONE
What specific things can you do as a leader to ensure social justice in your area of expertise?

_____

_____

_____

QUESTION TWO
On a scale of 1–10, how effective are you at ensuring social justice as a leader? Please explain why you chose this answer.

_____

_____

_____

QUESTION THREE
Based on your response to the previous rating, what specific things must you do in order to become more effective at ensuring social justice as a leader?

_____

_____

_____

QUESTION FOUR
What specific things can you do on a daily basis as a leader in order to ensure social justice in your area of expertise as a leader?

_____

_____

_____

LEADERSHIP QUESTION #38
Do you know how to walk by faith?

Dr. Martin Luther King Jr. once said, "Faith is taking the first step even when you don't see the whole staircase." I believe this an extremely powerful quote because men and women who live by their faith are willing to act upon principles they believe in, regardless of what the current situation may look like. In essence, a man or woman of faith will not only act upon the principles they believe in their heart to be true, but they fully believe that their present circumstance will change because of their ability to act upon the principles of faith that they possess. Moreover, leaders who walk by faith make history out of impossible situations because they have the faith to believe that impossible situations are not really impossible. Therefore, they act upon their principles of faith regardless of what the present situation make look like because their faith enables them to believe that invisible manifestations occur when people are willing to take that first step of faith without seeing the entire staircase.

Shockingly, although this is probably one of the most important characteristics of extraordinary leadership, it's rarely taught to individuals outside of spiritual circles. But when people understand how to walk by faith, the opportunities and impact that can be made by leaders is limitless because our faith creates invisible manifestations that would not occur if faith were not exercised. For example, in 1983, North Carolina State University shocked the world by beating the University of Houston in the NCAA Championship Game. Before the game began, not only was the University of Houston considered the top collegiate team, but everyone believed that North Carolina State University had no chance of winning the title. However, because of the faith that Jim Valvano and his extraordinary collegiate basketball team had in their basketball strategy, they were able to act upon this strategy that they all believed in and win the game. Similar to this illustration of the basketball strategy used by the North Carolina State University basketball team to win the game are the principles of success that we use in our lives to obtain amazing results regardless of the situation or circumstance. In order to see these principles of success manifest in our lives, we must have the faith and discipline to act upon these principles of success in any given situation.

As leaders of the twenty-first century, we may have different principles of faith that we believe in, but the positive results that will be obtained because of your faith will be based on your ability to act upon the principles of success that you believe are true. Now, before you start exercising your faith (speaking, thinking, and believing in something not visibly seen yet) and acting upon these principles of success that you believe are true, you want to make sure that they work and have produced results for other people throughout the years because you can experience failure with the wrong principles of success. Personally, I like to use the Bible as the foundational guide for the principles of success that I put my faith into because it is filled with an abundance of success principles that have produced positive results for me and other people I know for many years.

A great example of this manifestation occurred for me a few years ago when things became pretty slow in my speaking business and I seriously thought that my career was going to end. Instead of giving up on my dream because of my circumstance, I decided to exercise my faith and act upon some of my principles of success that I believe in as a speaker. Some of these principles of success that I used in my faith walk were morning prayer, daily affirmations over my speaking business, diligence and discipline with my day-to-day calls and emails, complete trust in God, positive thinking, positive speaking, continuous generosity with finances and other resources to others in need, and sensitivity to the intuitive thoughts that we all have an opportunity to receive every single day. Thankfully, after a couple of months of these intentional and daily activities, not only did my entire situation change, but I actually experienced one of the most profitable years of my speaking business ever. Personally, I believe it all happened because I exercised my faith and acted upon the right principles for success.

Ultimately, once you understand that walking by faith is about being able to *act upon* (not just believe) a set of principles of success that you believe are true, you will not only begin to see the amazing results that manifest because of your faith, but you will also discover that certain acts of faith cause invisible manifestations to occur in certain situations for you. And, once you understand this quality of spiritual leadership, you will begin to witness the limitless and extraordinary experiences that have occurred in the lives of many amazing leaders who have learned how to walk by faith.

To help you grow in this aspect of spiritual leadership, I have created a series of four questions for you to answer, develop, and discuss with your friends, mentors, and family members.

LEADERSHIP NOTES: _____

_____

_____

_____

_____

_____

_____

_____

_____

_____

_____

_____

_____

_____

_____

_____

_____

38

FOUR DISCUSSION QUESTIONS:
Do you know how to walk by faith?

QUESTION ONE

What specific things can you do as a leader to be more effective at walking by faith?

_____

_____

_____

QUESTION TWO

On a scale of 1–10, how effective are you at walking by faith as a leader? Please explain why you chose this answer.

_____

_____

_____

QUESTION THREE

Based on your response to the previous rating, what specific things must you do in order to become more effective at walking by faith as a leader?

_____

_____

_____

QUESTION FOUR

What specific things can you do on a daily basis in order to become more effective at walking by faith as a leader?

_____

_____

_____

LEADERSHIP QUESTION #39
Do you understand how to apply spiritual laws?

Approximately eleven years ago, I was a recent graduate who was unemployed and was searching for a job after attending college in the entertainment industry. For whatever reason, I was unable to find a job. So, I decided to take some time to pray and ask God to help me find a job. Shockingly, instead of creating a resume, attending a job fair, participating in a networking event, or calling some close contacts, it was impressed upon my heart to visit New York City. According to this gentle impression that I felt within, I really believed that God was telling me that a new job would manifest for me once I arrived in New York City. So I followed this gentle impression on the inside and booked a trip to New York City. As crazy as this story may sound, the moment I stepped foot off the plane in New York City, my phone rang and I was offered a new job the exact day that I was arriving back in Los Angeles. Now, this seemed to me like a coincidence at the time, but after seeing these types of experiences occurring in my life continuously over the past eleven years, I am fully convinced that there are certain spiritual laws in the universe that can help leaders attain positive results and reach their fullest potential.

Although I know that some leaders are not aware of these spiritual laws in the universe, I have discovered that there are other amazing leaders who have experienced great success because they have learned how to apply certain spiritual laws to their leadership journey. Even though I have many more spiritual laws to learn about in my lifetime, I would like to share with you a few spiritual laws that I believe will help you in your leadership journey. The first spiritual law that I have found to produce amazing results for me is the law of gratitude. In essence, instead of just focusing on the things you do not have yet, I believe it's important to be thankful and appreciative for the people, resources, blessings, and other amazing things that you already have in your life. Ultimately, when you consciously begin to give thanks for the things you do have, not only will you have more peace and happiness in your life, but it will open the door to new things in your life as well. This is why I believe Oprah Winfrey said, "Be thankful for what you do have, and you will end up having more."

The second spiritual law is the law of giving. The law of giving is defined differently by others, but the concept behind this law is that you reap what you sow. In essence, if you always treat people negatively, speak negatively, and do negative things, you are probably going to reap those negative things in a variety of different ways. However, if you are a giver of wisdom, money, love, and others positive energies, not only will you be blessed beyond your wildest imagination, but you will reap the rewards of it as well. Although it took some time for me to learn the power of this concept as it relates to my finances, over time I have found that the more I have given financially in a responsible manner, the more I have received in ways I could never have imagined.

The third and final spiritual law that I would like to share with you is the Law of Attraction. The Law of Attraction demonstrates how we create the things, events, and people that come into our lives through our thoughts, feelings, and words. Even though there are some who disagree with this concept, I am a strong believer in words and thoughts having a huge impact on the types of things that we produce in our lives. In essence, if you think and speak negatively about a variety of different things in your life, chances are you're going to see that manifest. But if you speak and think positively, you are more likely to see the manifestation of positive things in your life. So, as a leader in the twenty-first century, it's important that you discipline your language and watch your thoughts carefully because they can have an effect on your success as a leader. Personally, I think this is why some people have always said, "Be careful what you ask for because you might actually receive it."

Obviously, there are many other spiritual laws that can help us reach our fullest potential as leaders of the twenty-first century, but these are a few of the spiritual laws that have helped me and can help you become more effective as a leader. As you continue to grow in this aspect of your leadership, I encourage you to learn about some of the other spiritual laws of the universe as well because they will surely empower you to do some amazing things as a leader.

To help you grow in this aspect of spiritual leadership, I have created a series of four questions for you to answer, develop, and discuss with your friends, mentors, and family members.

LEADERSHIP NOTES: _____

_____

_____

_____

_____

_____

_____

_____

_____

_____

_____

_____

_____

_____

_____

_____

_____

_____

39

FOUR DISCUSSION QUESTIONS:
Do you understand how to apply spiritual laws?

QUESTION ONE

What specific things can you do to be more effective at applying spiritual laws as a leader?

_____

_____

_____

QUESTION TWO

On a scale of 1–10, how effective are you at applying spiritual laws as a leader? Please explain why you chose this answer.

_____

_____

_____

QUESTION THREE

Based on your response to the previous rating, what specific things must you do in order to become more effective at applying spiritual laws as a leader?

_____

_____

_____

QUESTION FOUR

What specific things can you do on a daily basis in order to become more effective at applying spiritual laws as a leader?

_____

_____

_____

LEADERSHIP QUESTION #40
Do you have a relationship with god?

Over the past decade, there has been a unique trend among members of the younger generation (those born between 1977–2000), which is that instead of young men and women who believe in God stating that they are religious, they are stating more than ever that they are spiritual. Some experts believe that one of the main reasons that 72% of members of the younger generation are stating that they are more spiritual than religious is because many of these young men and women are rejecting the notion that traditional organized religion is the sole or most valuable means of furthering spiritual growth. Whether or not you agree with this new movement, one thing is true: More and more men and women of this younger generation are realizing that spirituality is not just about religious ceremonies, traditions, and denominations—it's also about having a personal relationship with God. Although people's belief in God is different among various leaders all around the world, the reality is that if you are going to see the impact of your spirituality as it relates to leadership, you must have a personal relationship with God.

Even though people's relationship with God varies based on one's religious or spiritual beliefs, I have found that having a personal relationship with God means that you pray daily, you ask God questions daily, you seek God for answers, you talk to God about your problems, you ask God for direction in certain situations, you allow God to order your steps and help you make important decisions in life, you spend time with God, and most importantly, you take the time each day to develop and enhance your relationship with God as you would a friend, family member, or significant other. Thankfully, after building my personal relationship with God over the past twenty-five years, I have discovered that having a relationship with God has not only provided me with comfort in the most challenging situations as a leader, but this awesome relationship that I have developed with God has also been a strong catalyst toward helping me obtain personal, career, and leadership success.

One example that really stands out to me occurred a couple of years ago when I almost lost my entire speaking career because I was unable to secure any speaking engagements for almost four months. Even though I had been working regularly as a national speaker for almost five years, there was a moment in my career when I was not receiving any calls at all, and my financial situation was looking very bad. In addition to these challenges with my business, my rent was raised, I had two car accidents, and I was in the process of trying to publish my fourth book, which required money. At that point in my career, I thought it was going to end and figured it was time for me to pursue a regular 9-to-5 job. But, thankfully, because of my relationship with God, instead of allowing these negative circumstances to affect me, I began to seek God for answers to these problems. And, within days, not only did I receive some answers to my situation, but I applied some of the spiritual principles that were impressed upon my heart in prayer to my current situation and saw my entire negative situation turn into a positive one within months. Moreover, just four months after this challenging time with my speaking business, I actually made more money than I had even expected that year. Although there were many powerful lessons that I was able to learn from this experience, the most impactful lesson that I learned during that time is that God always has the answer to your most challenging situations as a leader, if you're willing to ask about it, and that your greatest achievements as a leader normally come right after your greatest trials and tribulations in life.

As you move forward in your leadership journey, I encourage you to develop a personal relationship with God because it really does make a huge difference. To help you grow in this aspect of spiritual leadership, I have created a series of four questions for you to answer, develop, and discuss with your friends, mentors, and family members.

LEADERSHIP NOTES: _____

_____

_____

_____

_____

_____

_____

_____

_____

_____

_____

_____

_____

_____

_____

_____

_____

FOUR DISCUSSION QUESTIONS:
Do you have a relationship with god?

QUESTION ONE

What specific things can you do as a leader to develop a stronger relationship with God?

_____

_____

_____

QUESTION TWO

On a scale of 1–10, how strong of a relationship do you have with God as it relates to your leadership experience? Please explain why you chose this answer.

_____

_____

_____

QUESTION THREE

Based on your response to the previous rating, what specific things must you do as a leader in order to develop a stronger relationship with God?

_____

_____

_____

QUESTION FOUR

What specific things can you do on a daily basis as a leader in order to become more effective at developing a stronger relationship with God?

_____

_____

_____

ABOUT AUTHOR

JOSHUA
FREDENBURG

Joshua Fredenburg is a national speaker, author, entrepreneur, television commentator, and leadership/diversity/generational expert that specializes in current issues and effective leadership strategies for emerging and seasoned leaders. For the past six years, Joshua has served as a dynamic keynote speaker in 40 different states for various leadership conferences, retreats and trainings at high schools, colleges and organizations across the country.

In addition to speaking and empowering emerging and seasoned leaders for leadership success, Joshua has also written three books, completed an MA in Organizational Leadership, spoken on a variety of television shows as an expert on issues pertaining to Generation Y and has developed an annual leadership conference that prepares college students and young professionals for executive level leadership positions after graduation and brings together over 50 senior executives from major corporations. Currently, Joshua also serves as a board member for the Lois Swanson Leadership Center at California State University, Long Beach, writes a popular monthly newsletter that reaches 10,000 people on issues that revolve around leadership, is pursuing a PhD in Organizational Leadership and serves as mentor and coach to various emerging and seasoned leaders throughout the country.

As a keynote speaker, Joshua has been well received by a variety of different audiences for his amazing energy, inspiring and engaging messages, insightful wisdom and knowledge about leadership and his strong commitment to helping emerging and seasoned leaders become great leaders of the 21st Century. He has also been very popular amongst high school and college audiences because of his positive attitude, exciting presentations, authentic message and his strong ability to connect and make his message relatable to diverse audiences throughout the country.

Made in the USA
Columbia, SC
18 February 2020